This awesome book belongs to this awesome child

_____

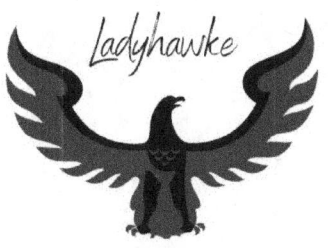

Copyrighted 2022
Ladyhawke Publications
All Rights Reserved

Count & Color

What number do you see and how many animals do you count? Is it correct?

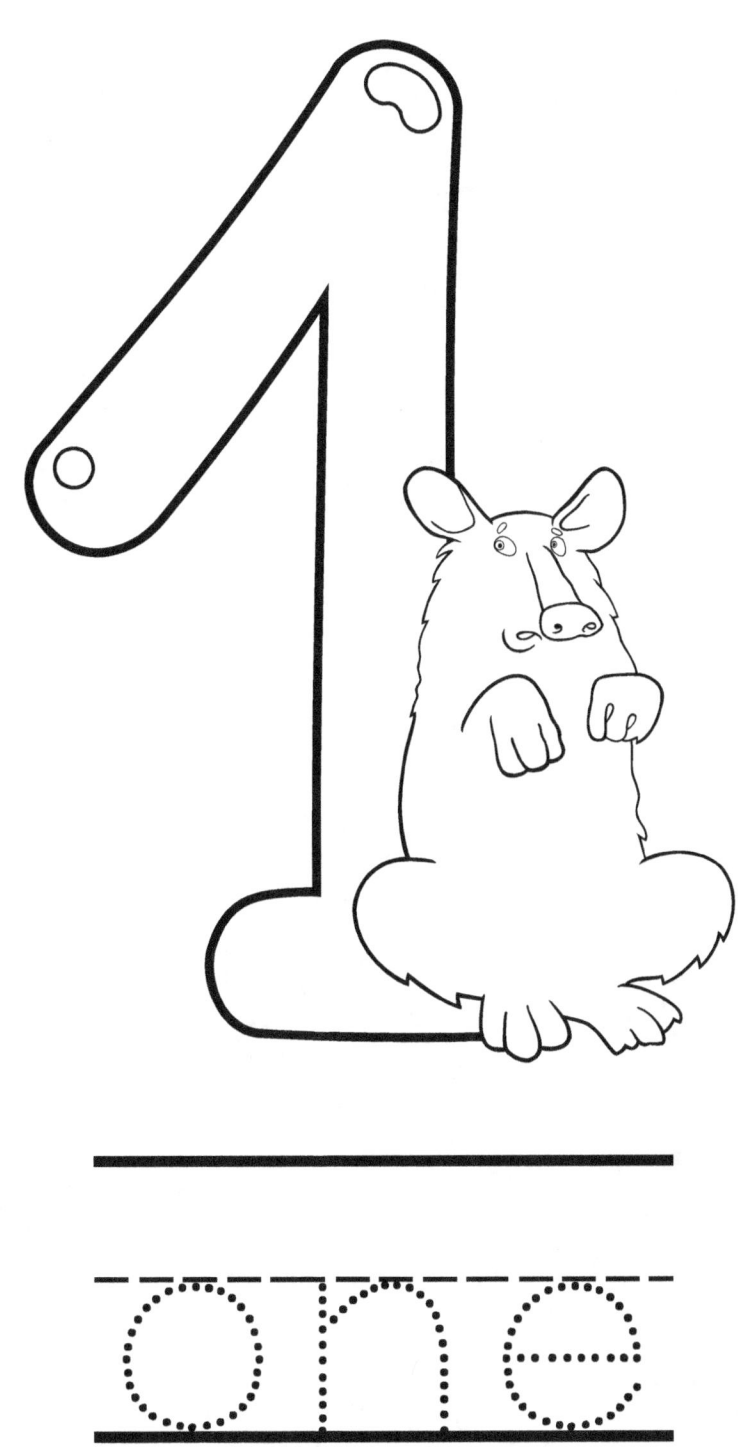

Count & Color

What number do you see and how many animals do you count? Is it correct?

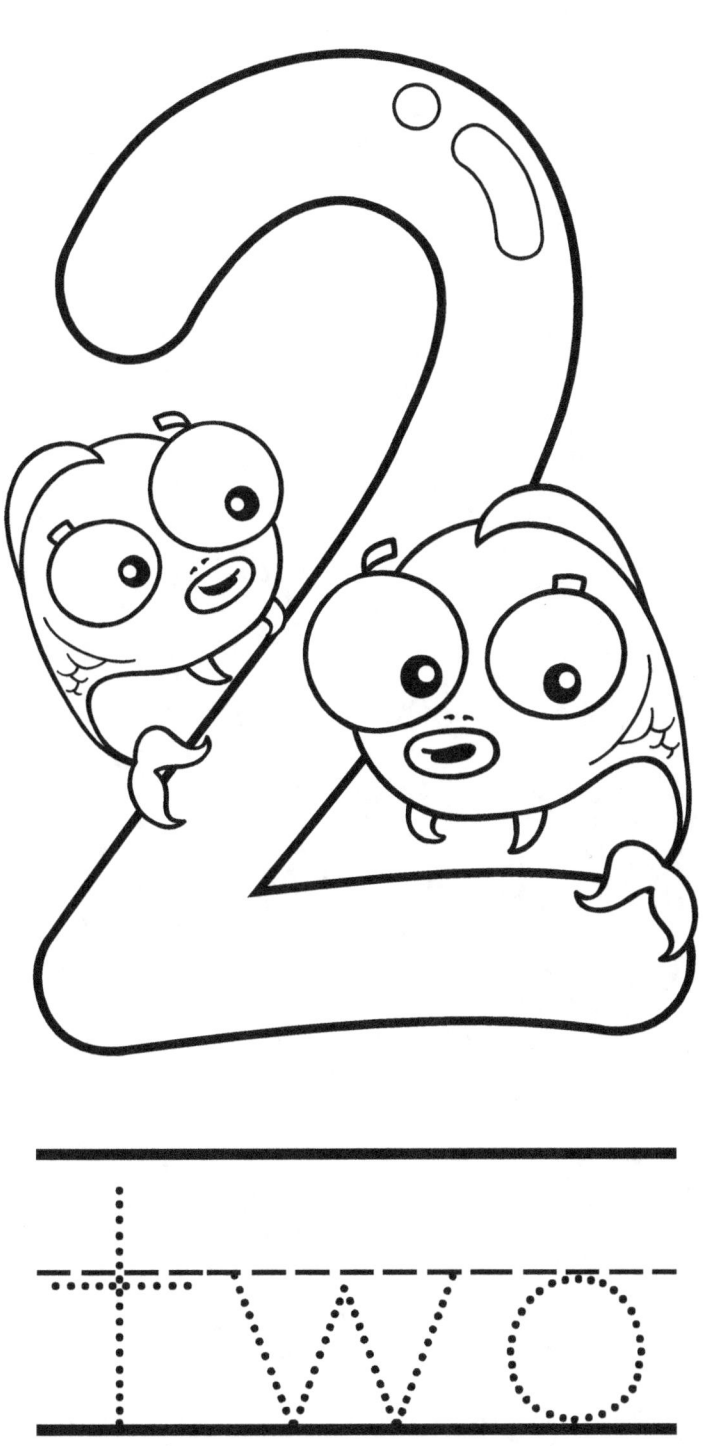

two

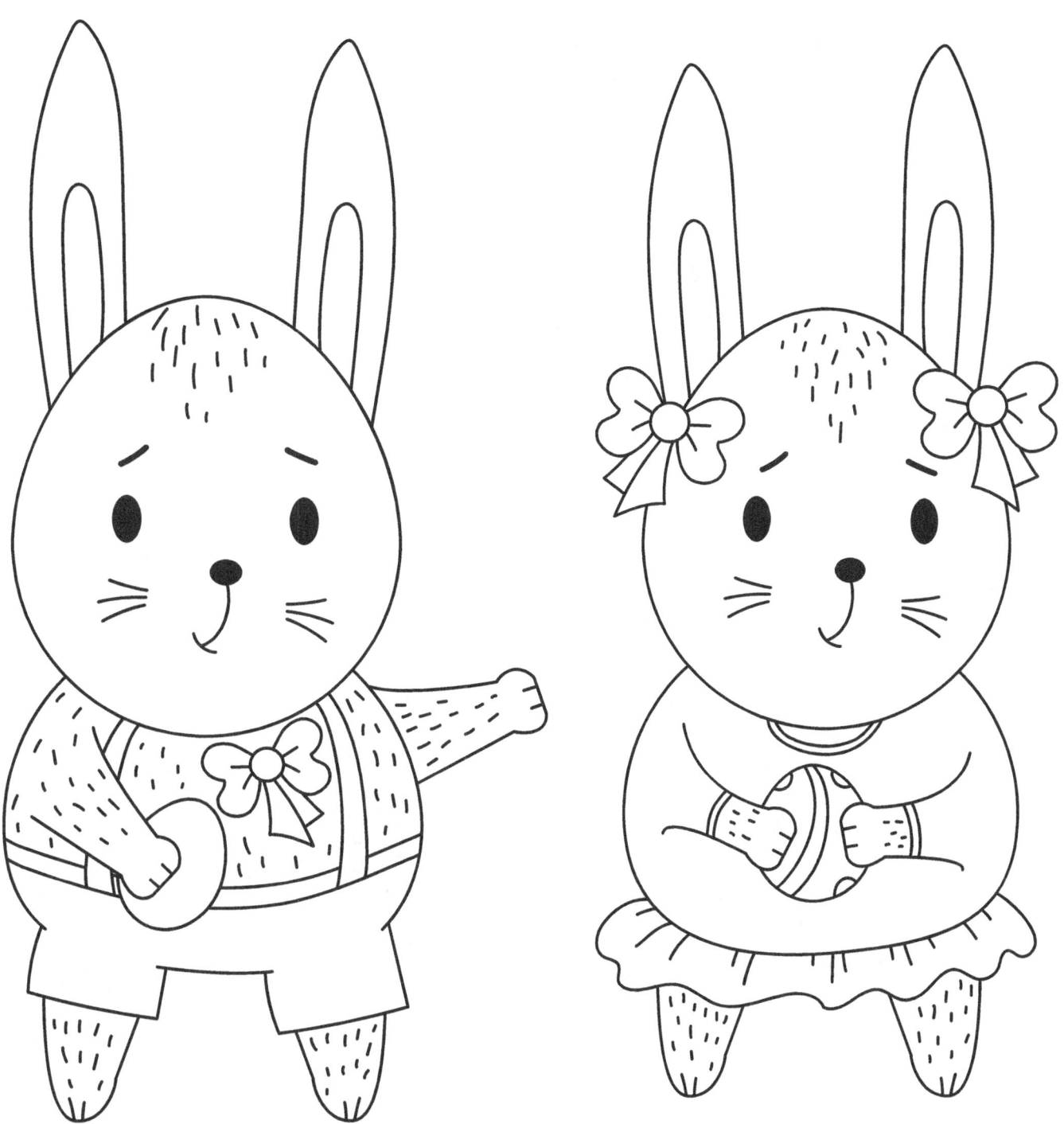

Count & Color

What number do you see and how many animals do you count? Is it correct?

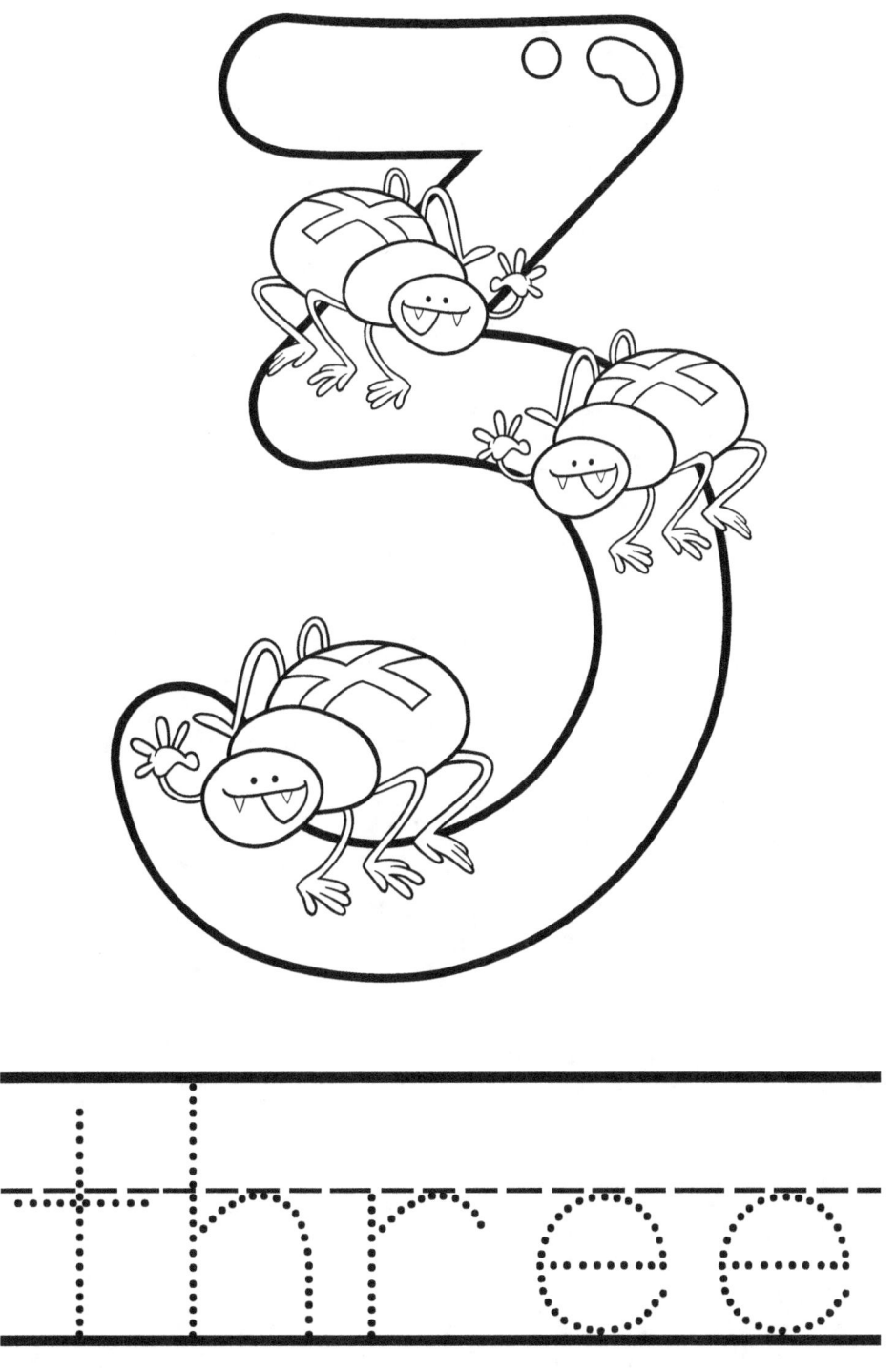

three

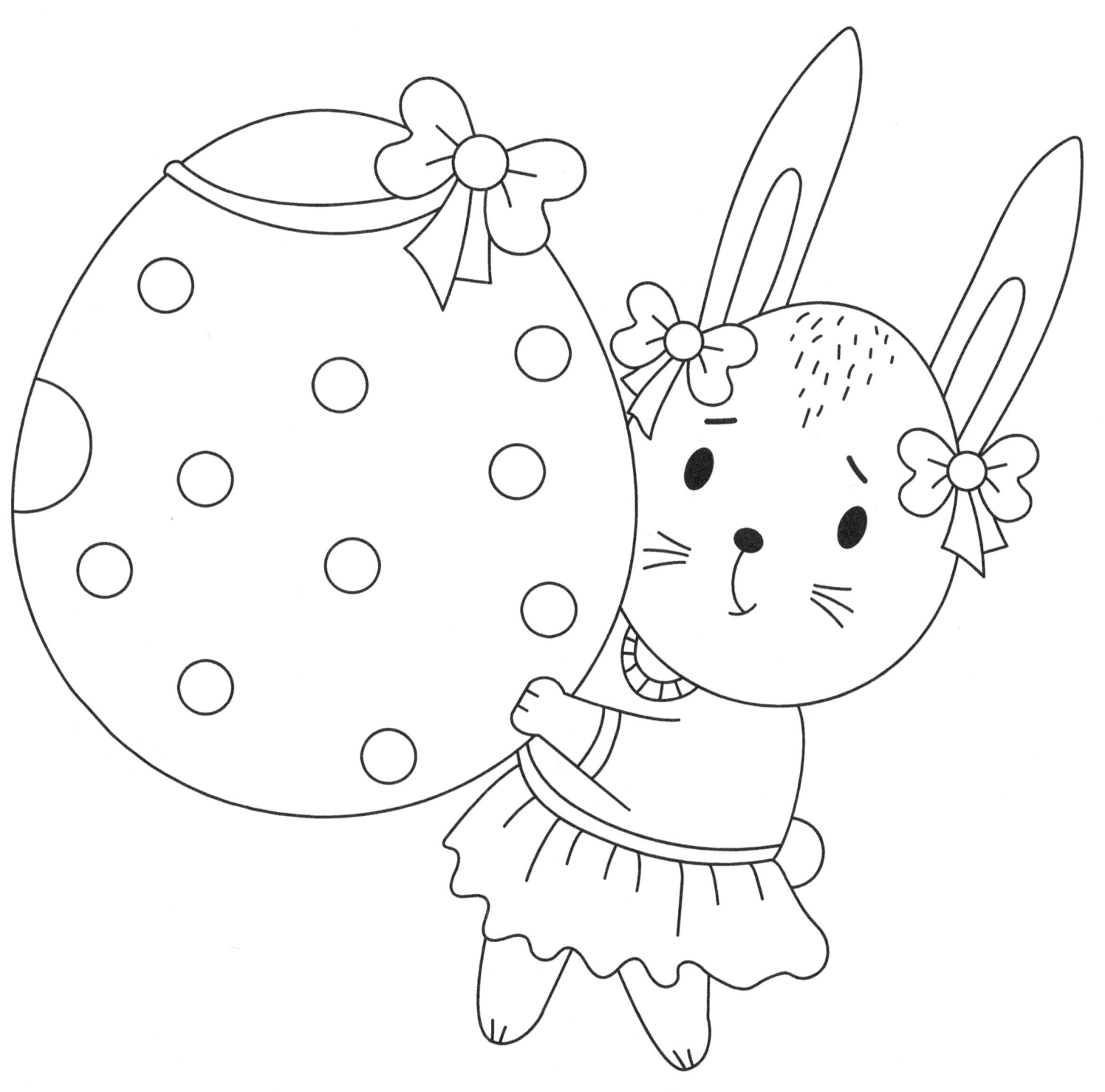

Count & Color

What number do you see and how many animals do you count? Is it correct?

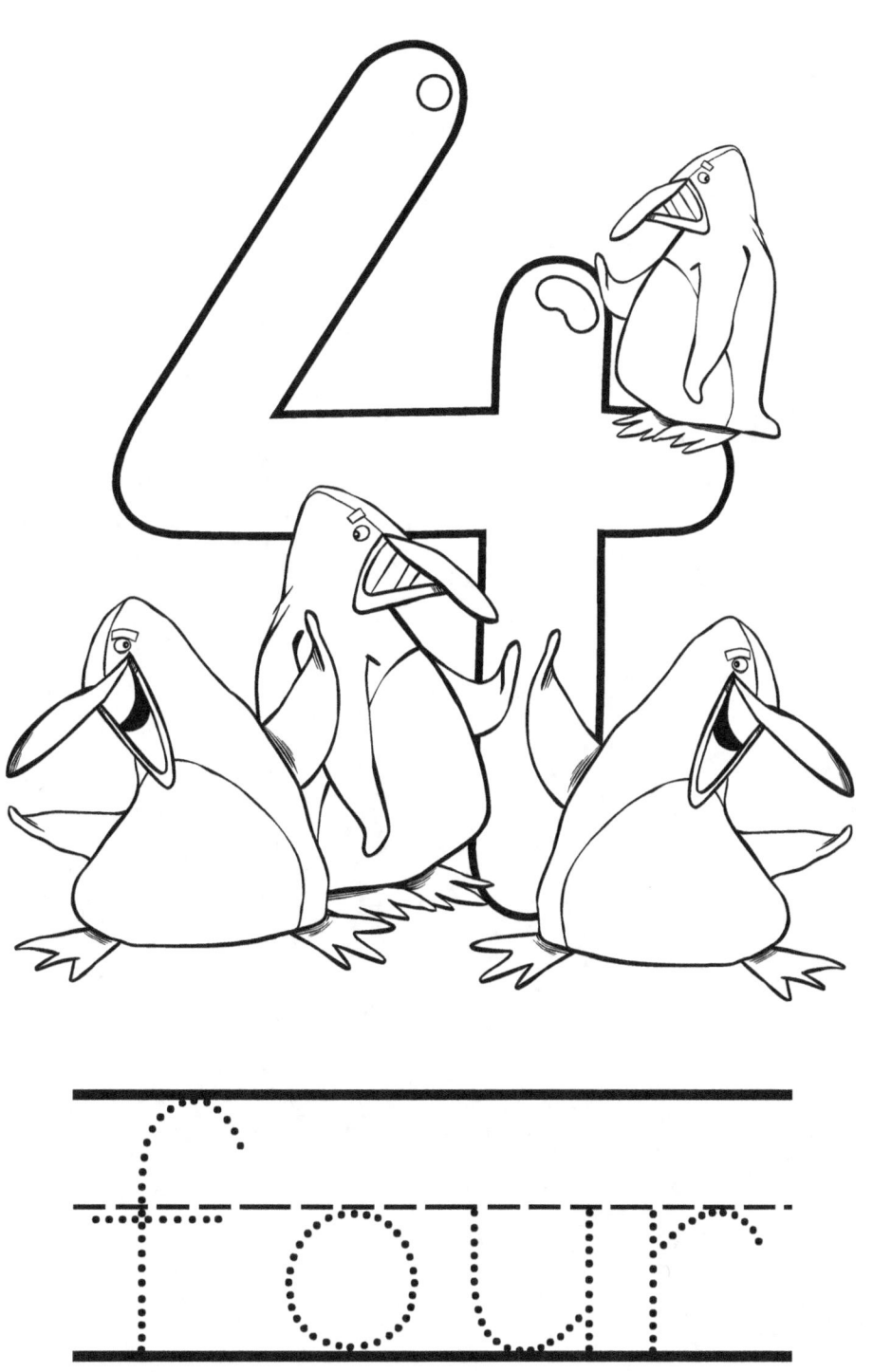

four

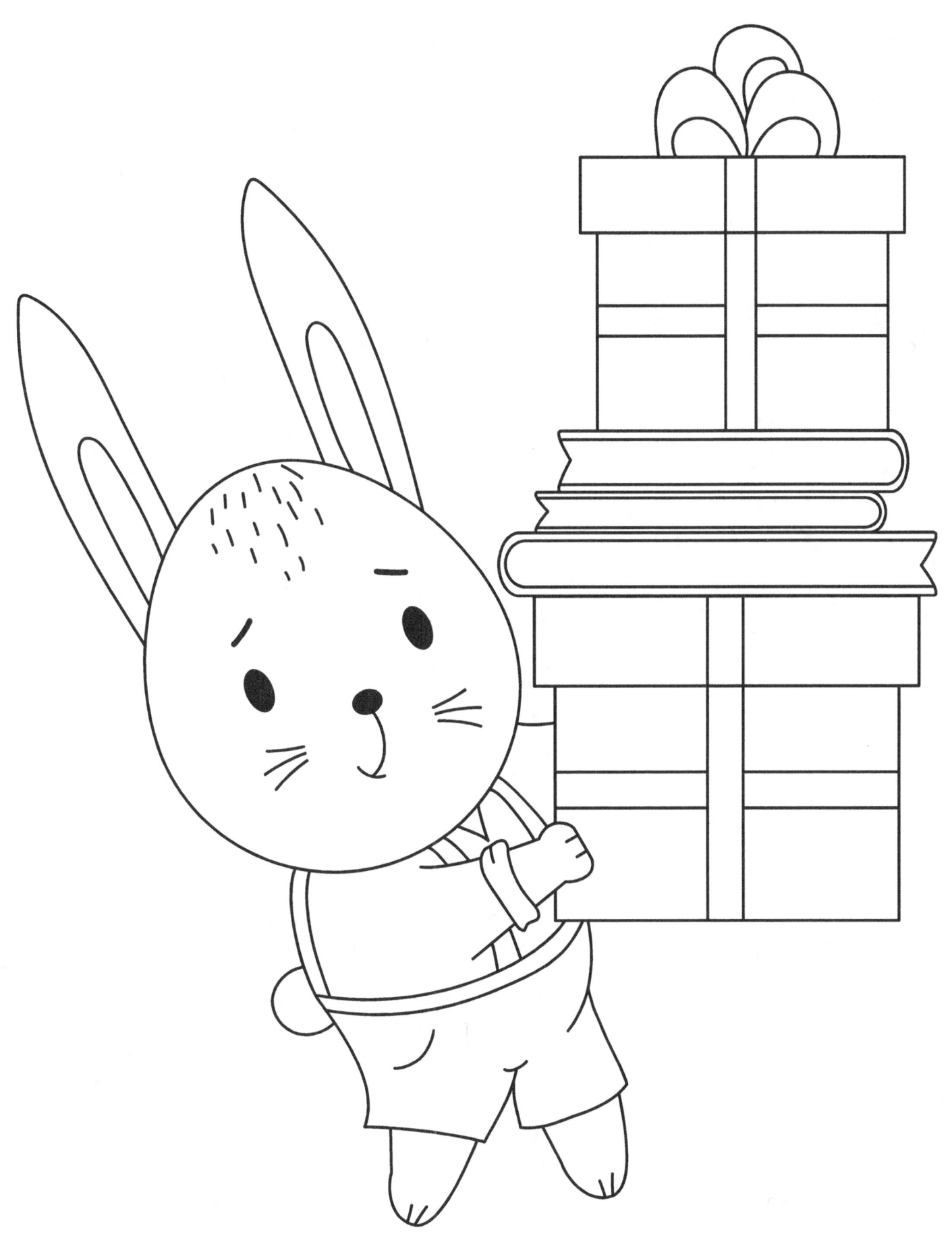

Count & Color

What number do you see and how many animals do you count? Is it correct?

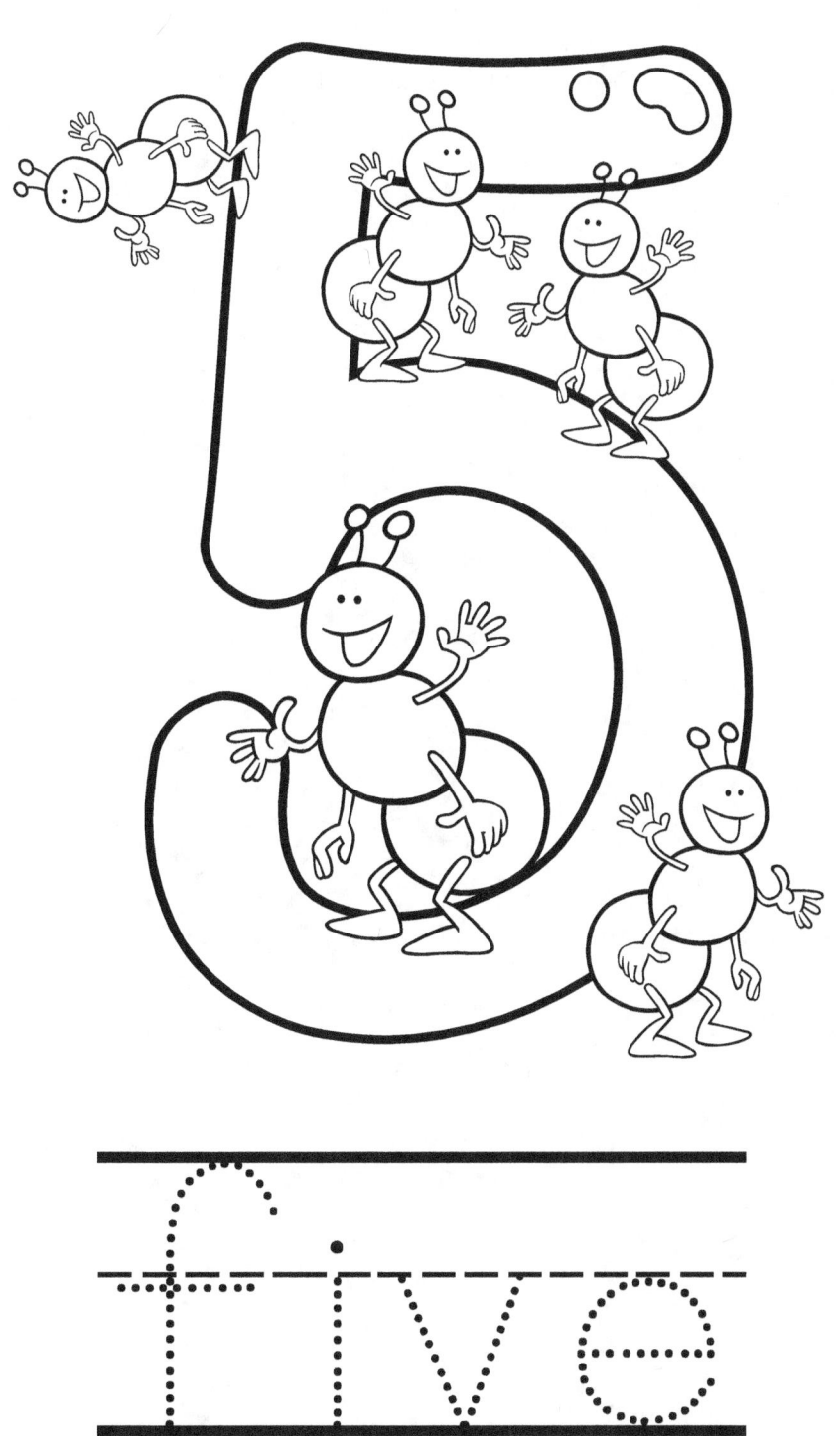

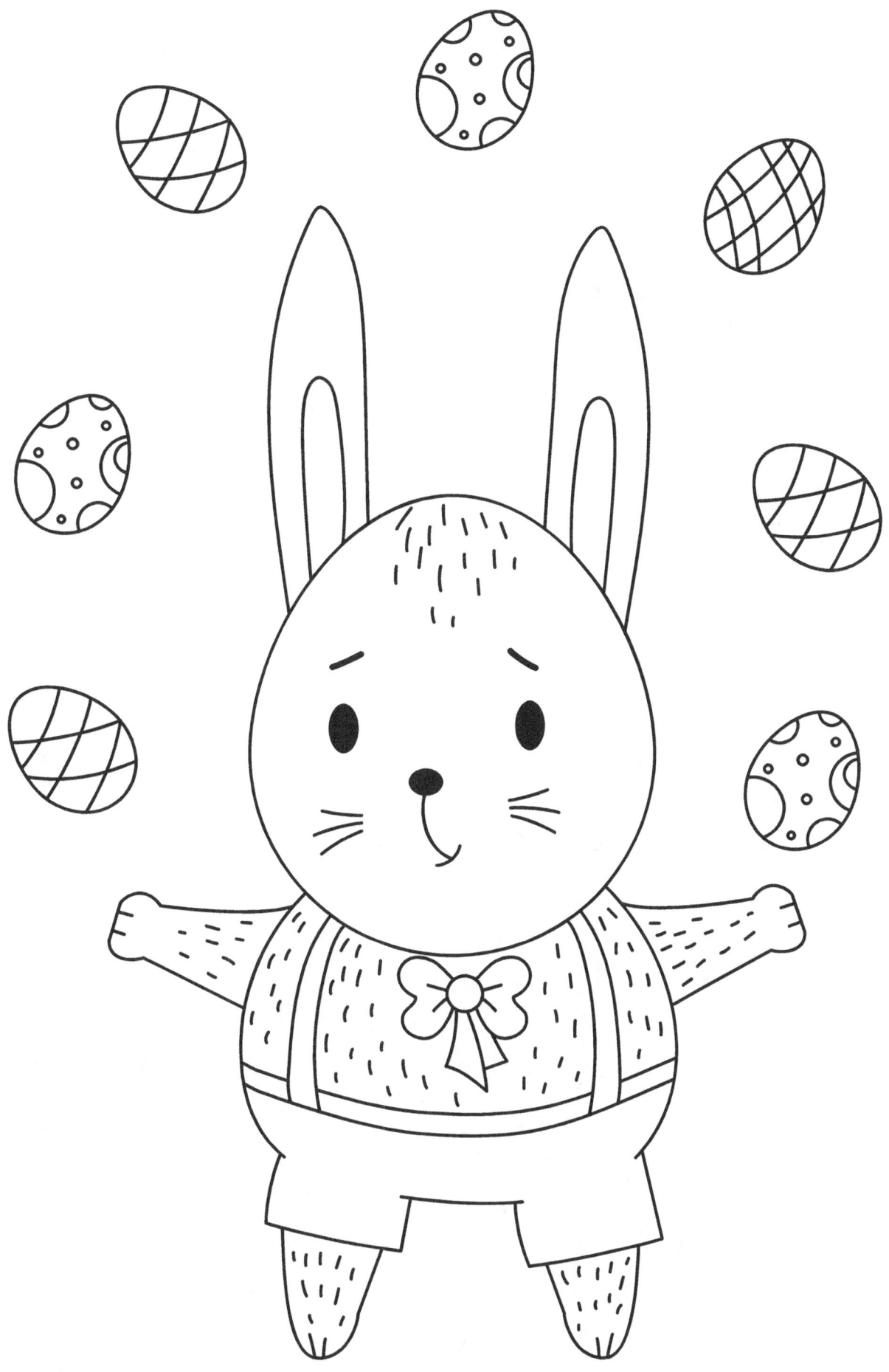

Count & Color

What number do you see and how many animals do you count? Is it correct?

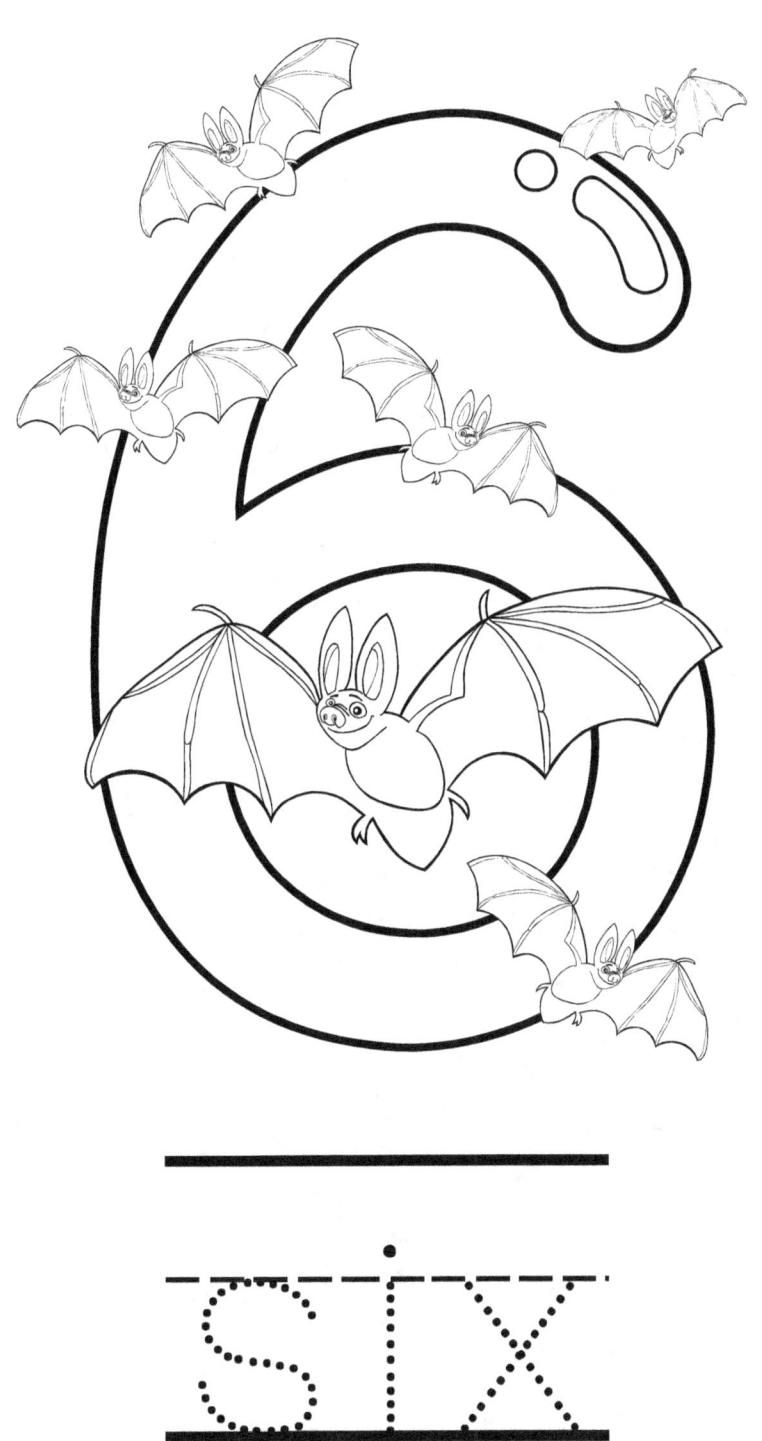

six

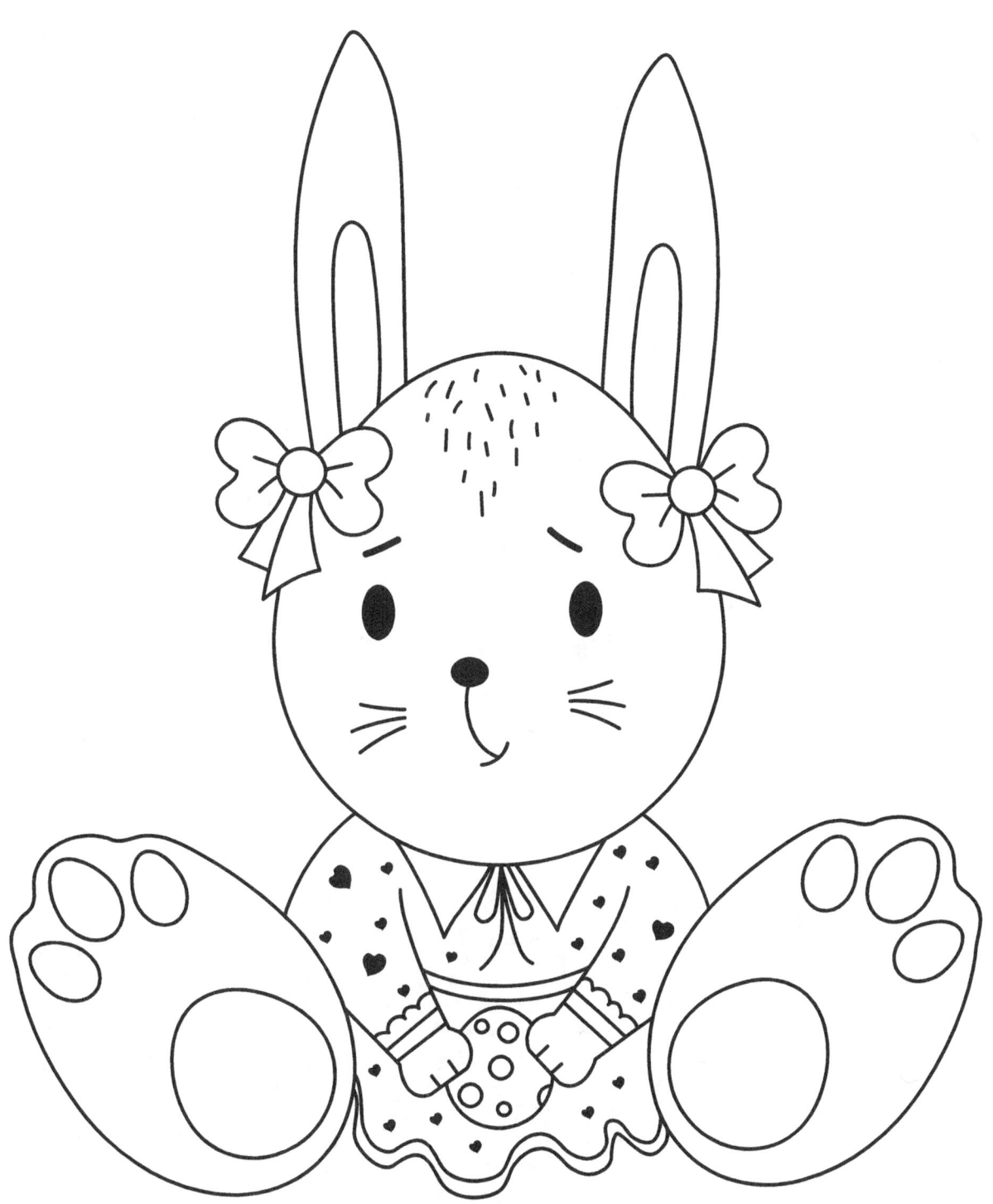

Count & Color

What number do you see and how many animals do you count? Is it correct?

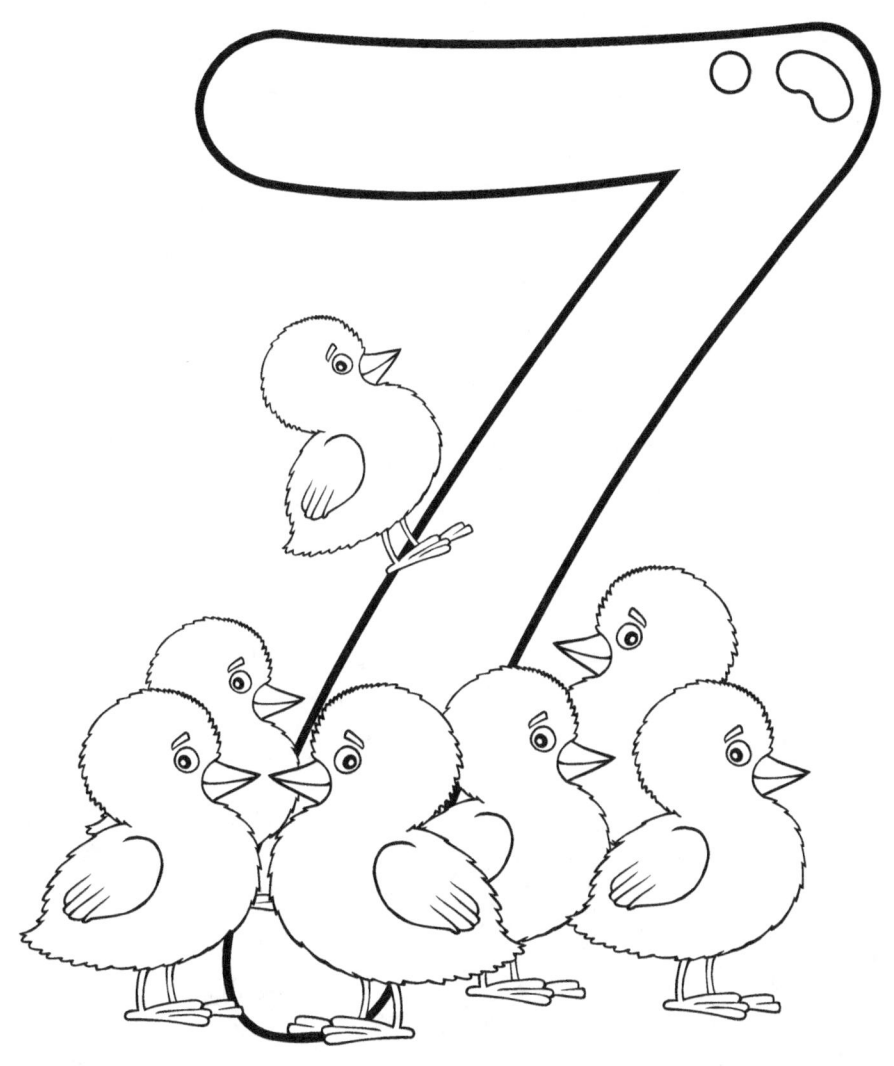

seven

Count & Color

What number do you see and how many animals do you count? Is it correct?

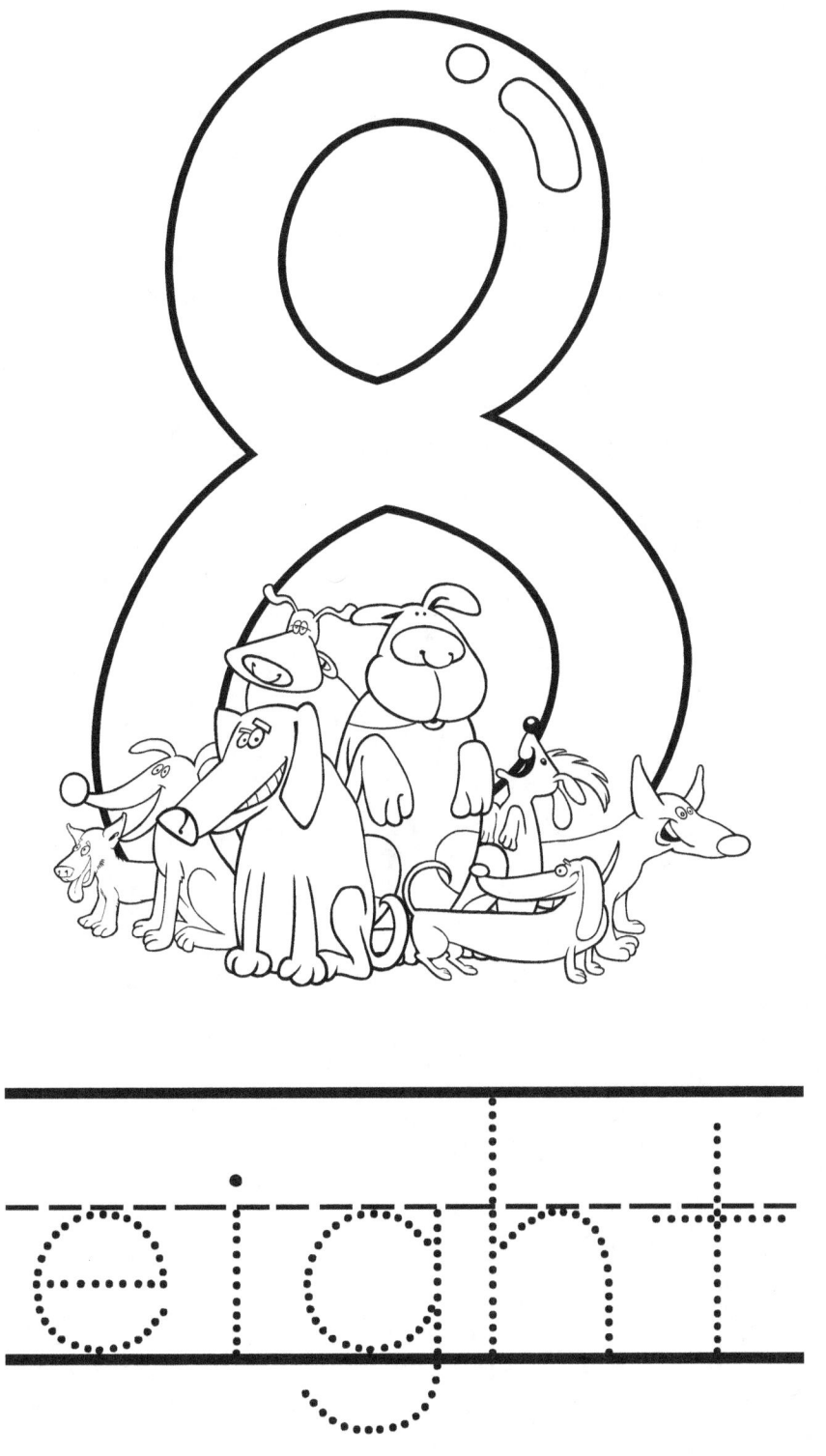

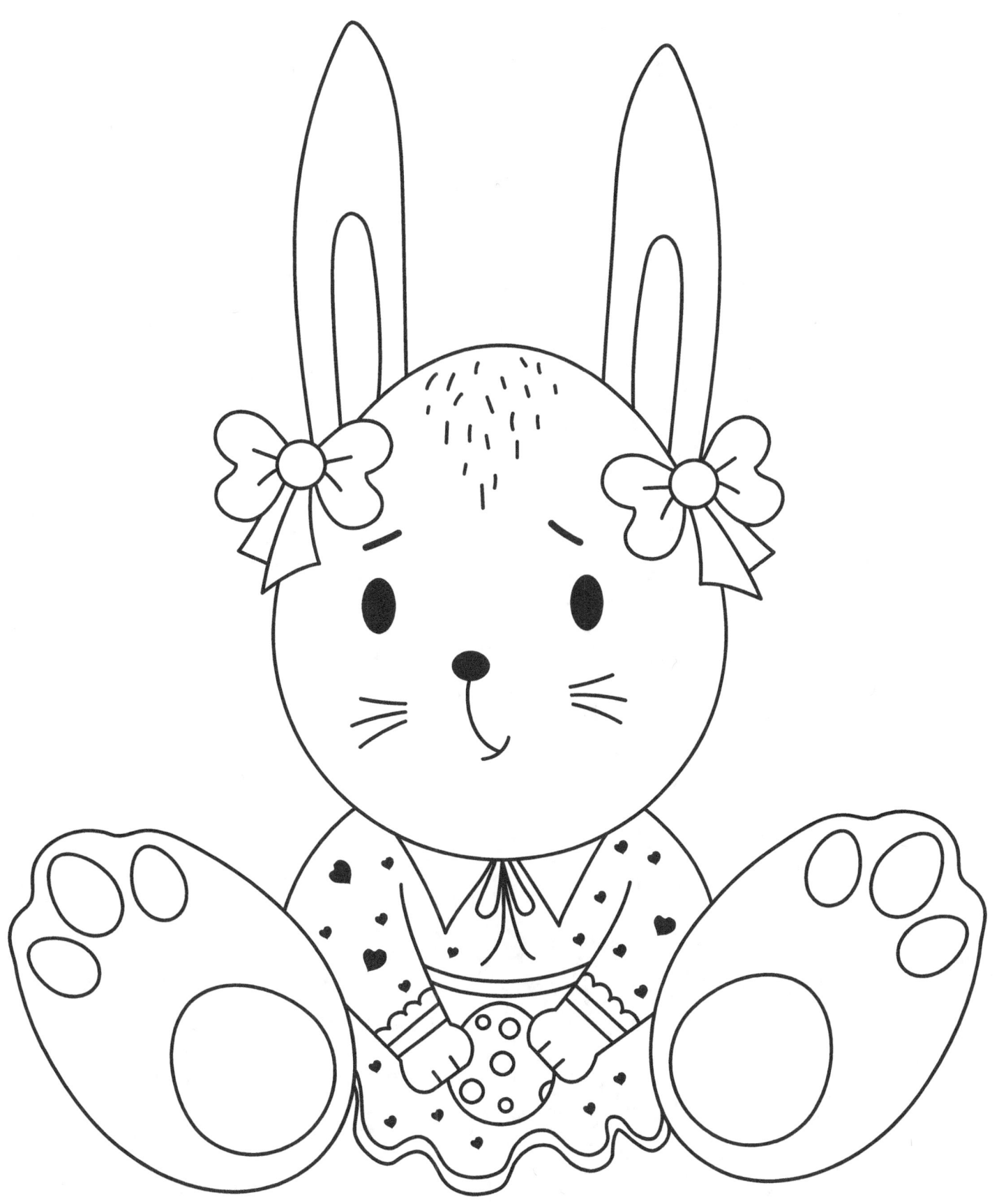

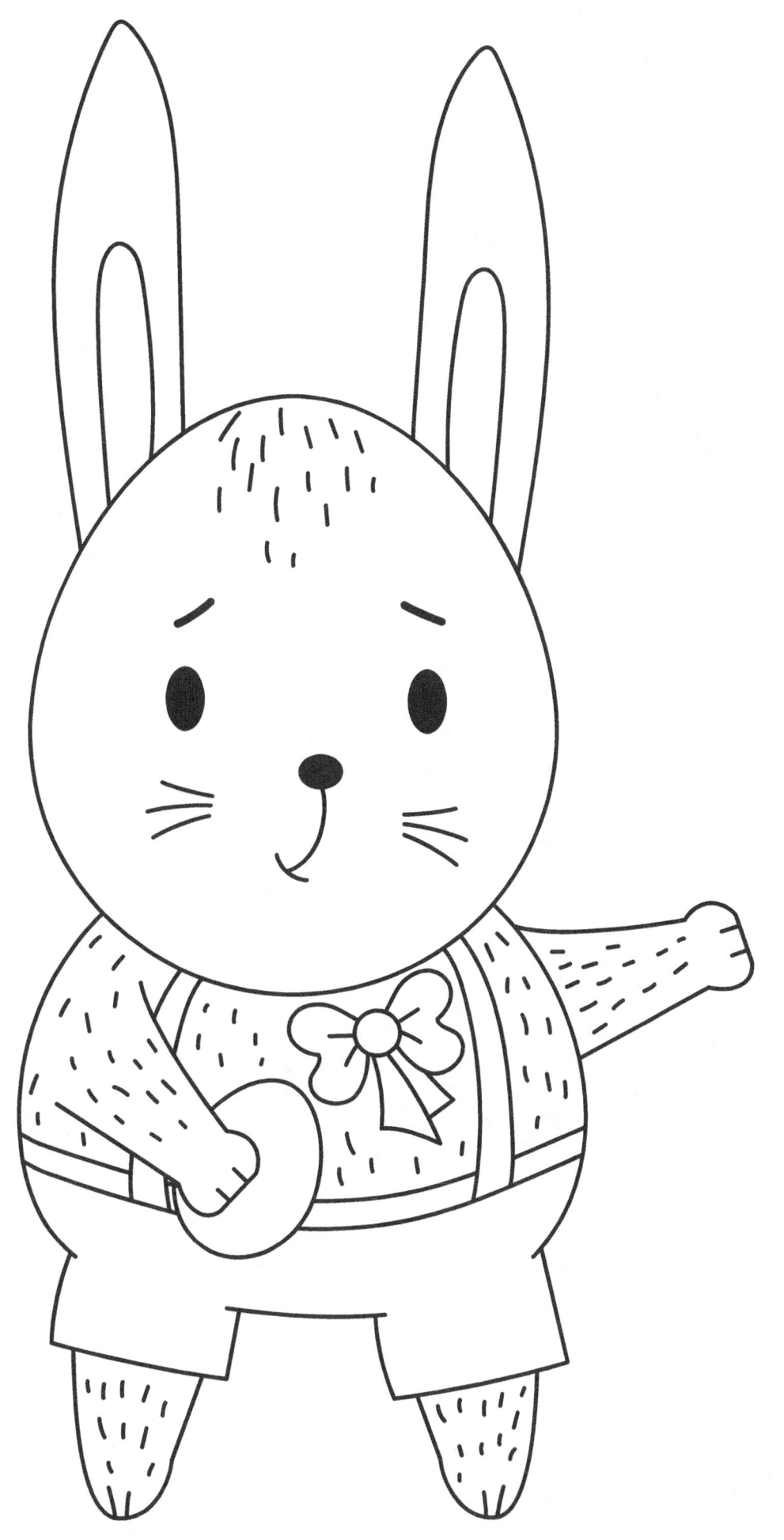

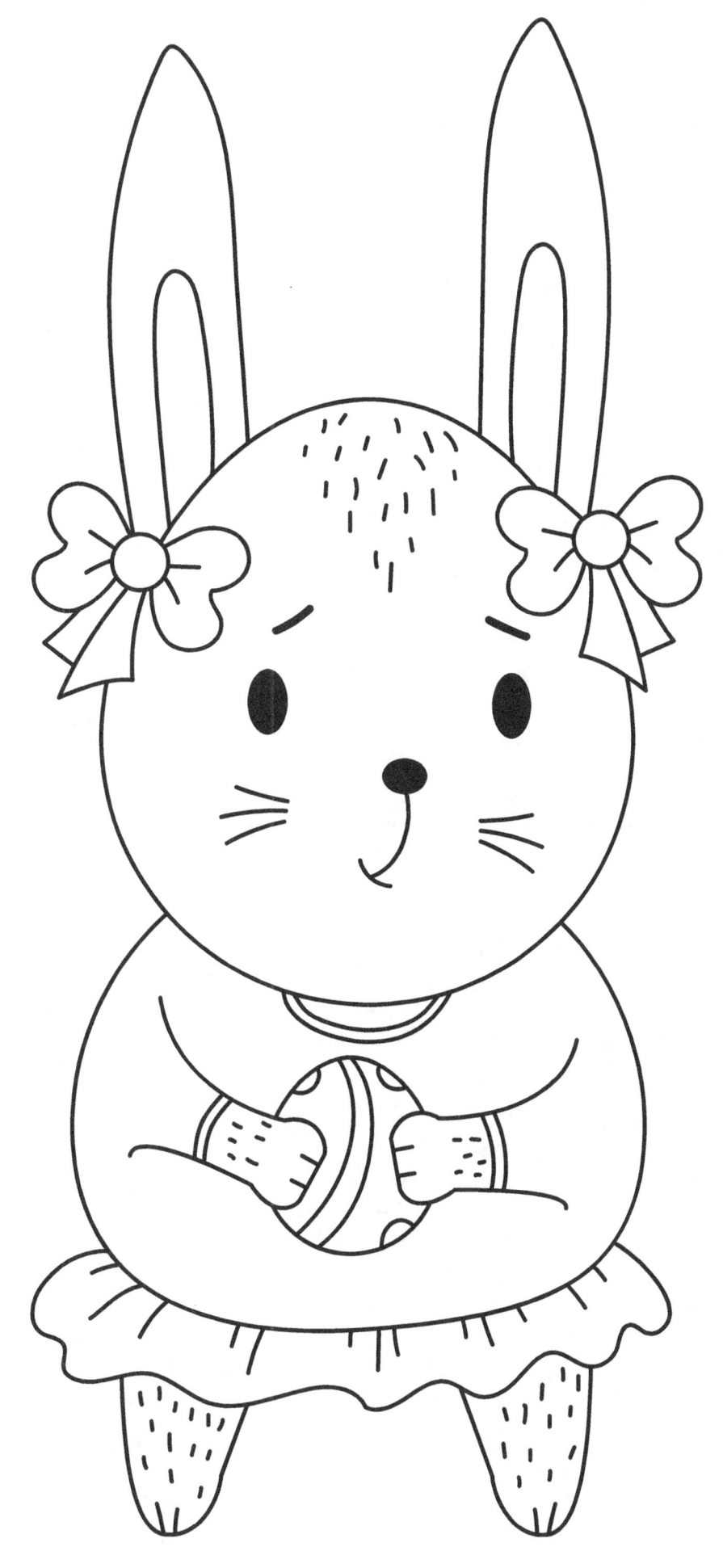

Count & Color

What number do you see and how many animals do you count? Is it correct?

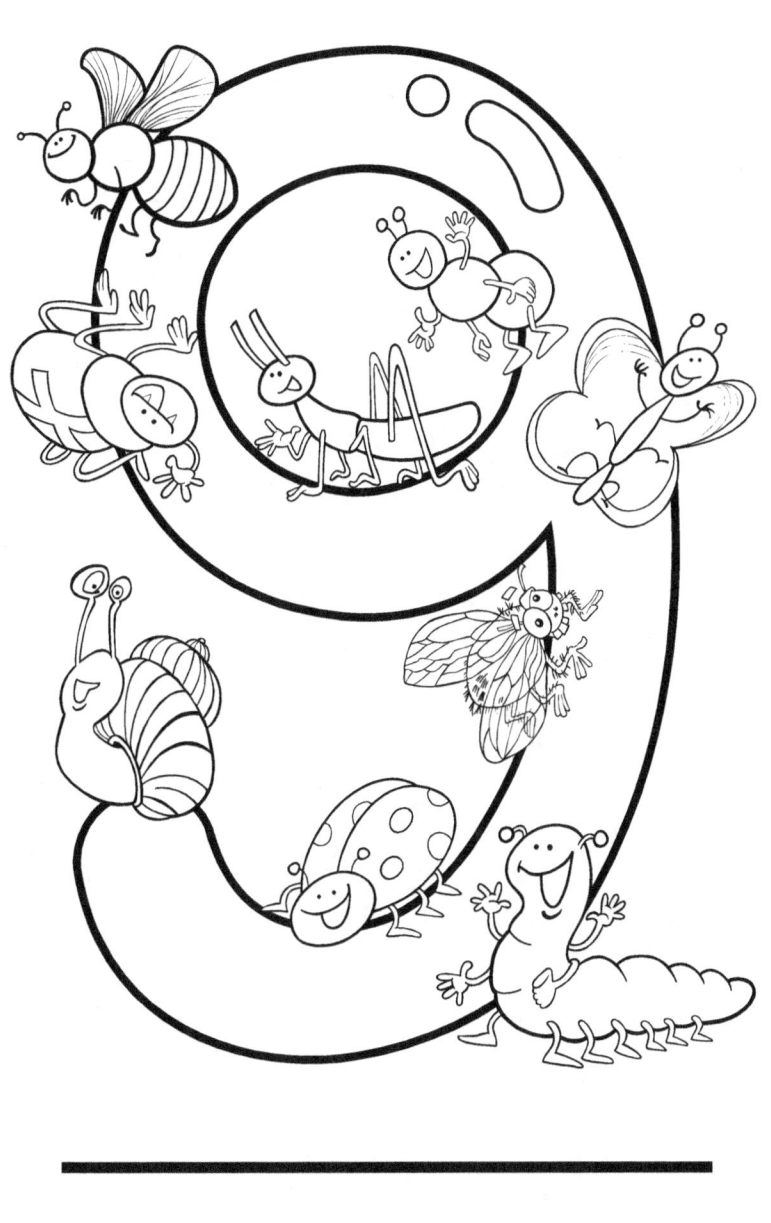

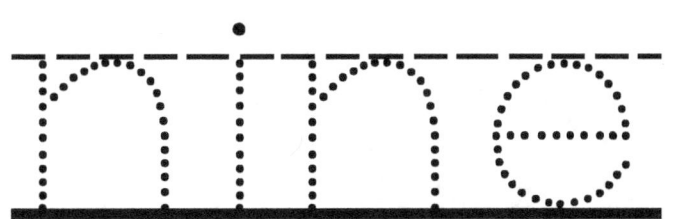

Count & Color

What number do you see and how many animals do you count? Is it correct?

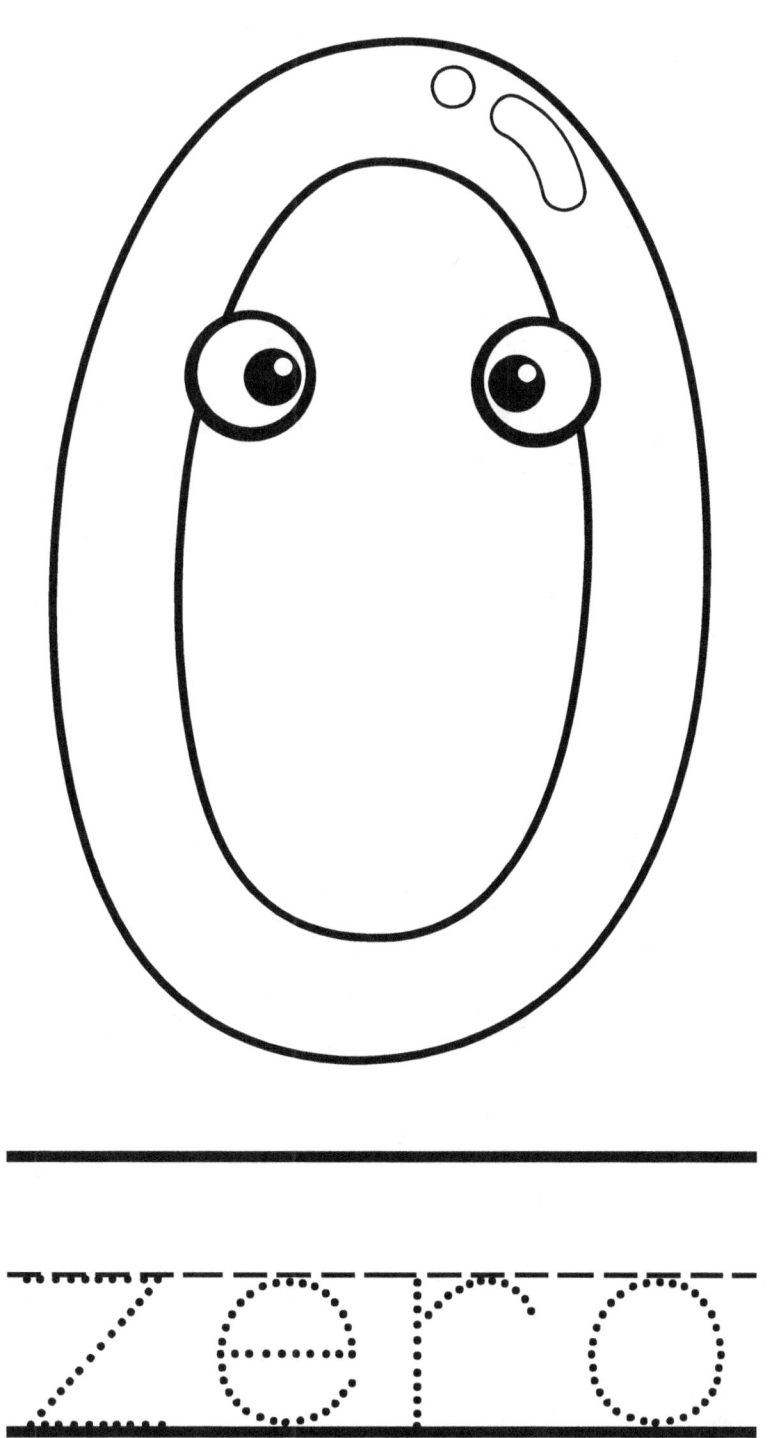

zero

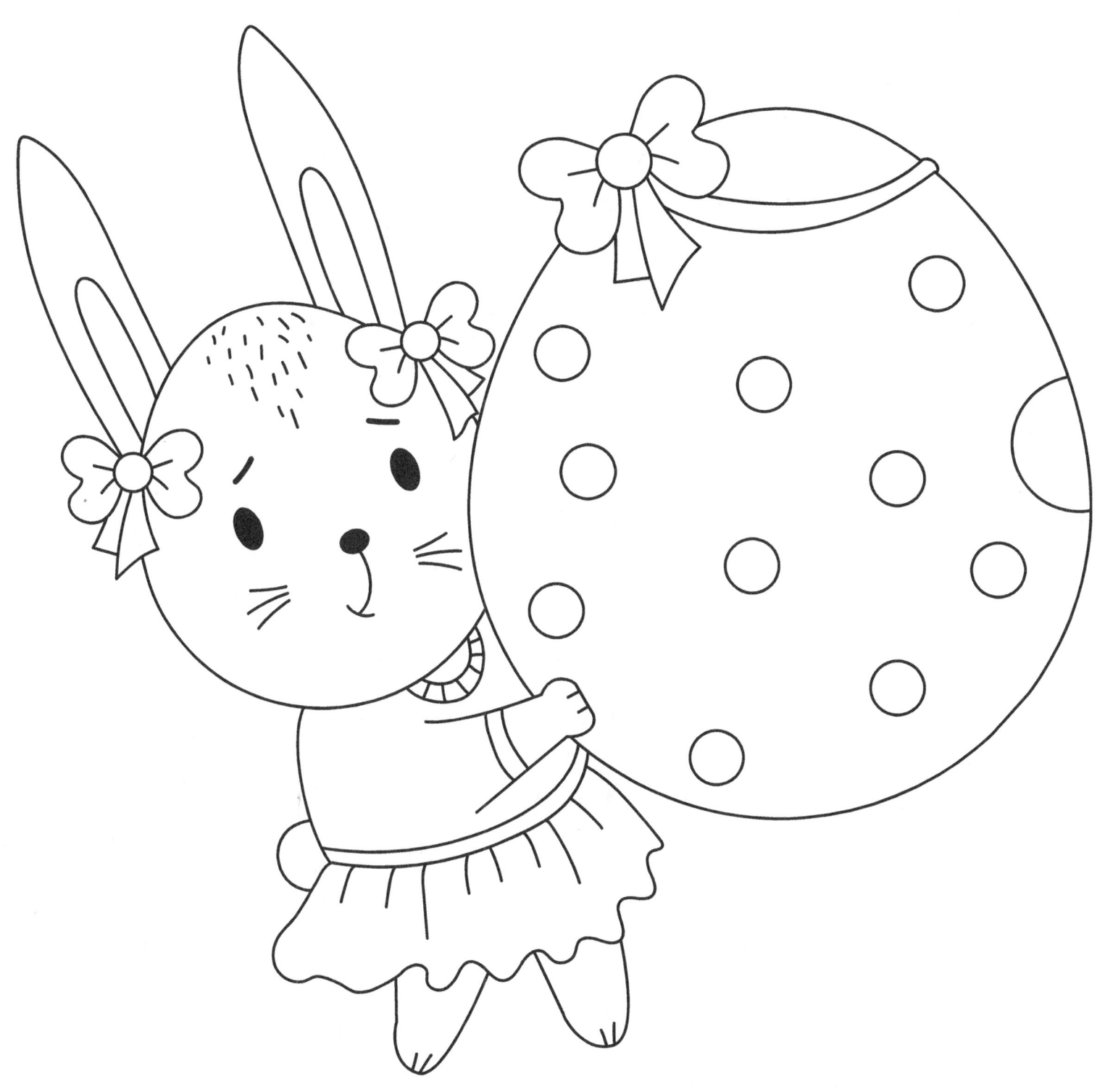

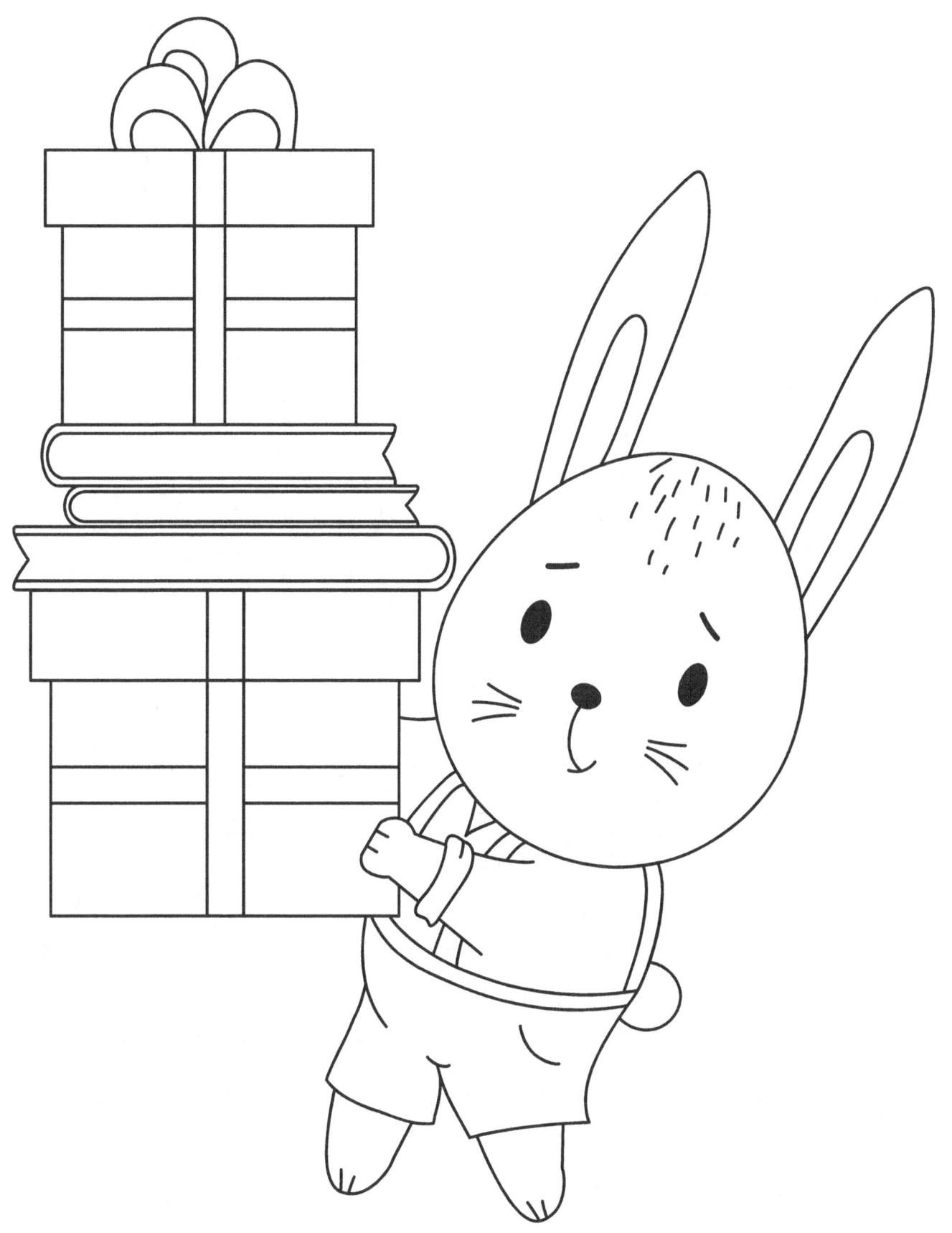

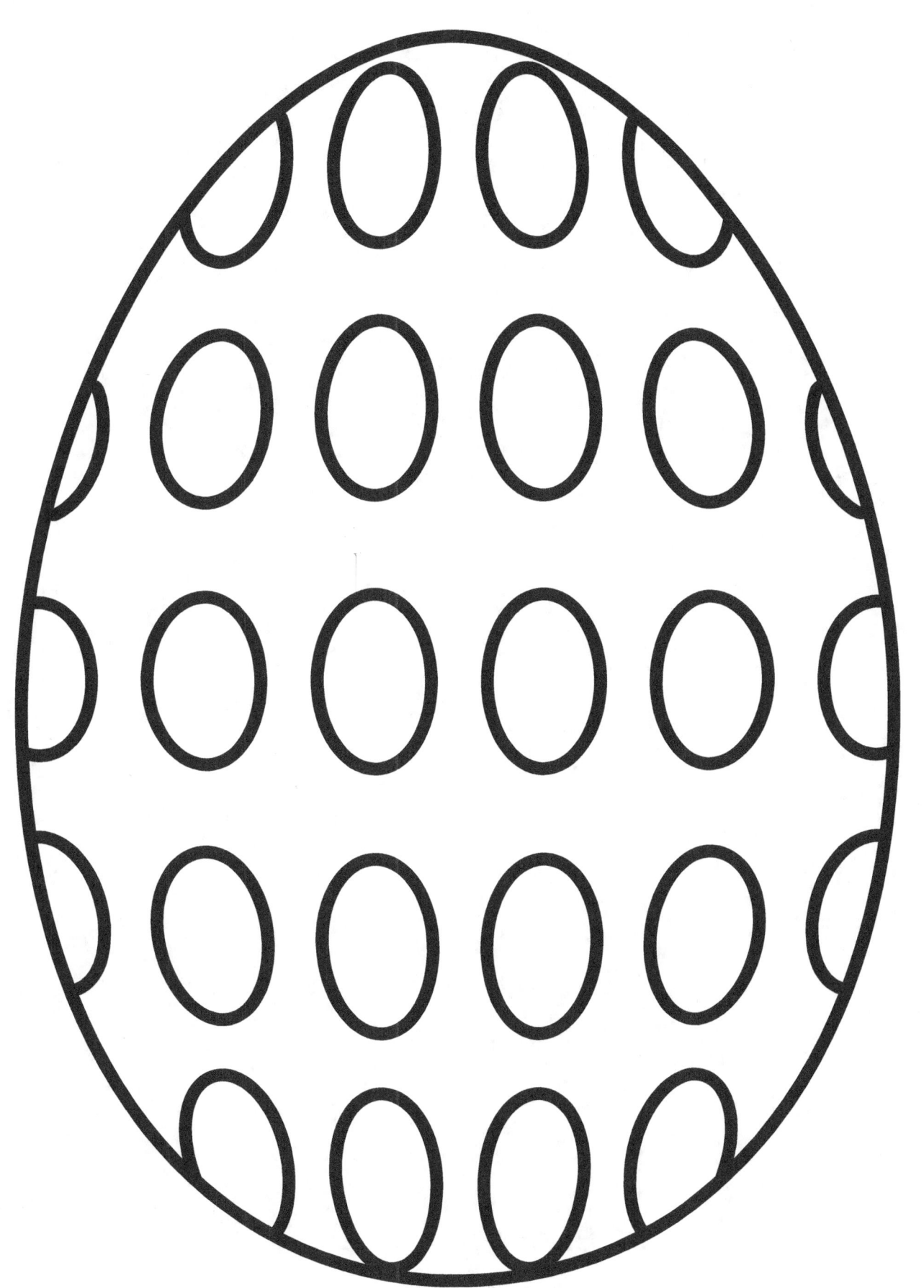

Count & Mark

Count and color the Easter elements in each box, mark the correct number

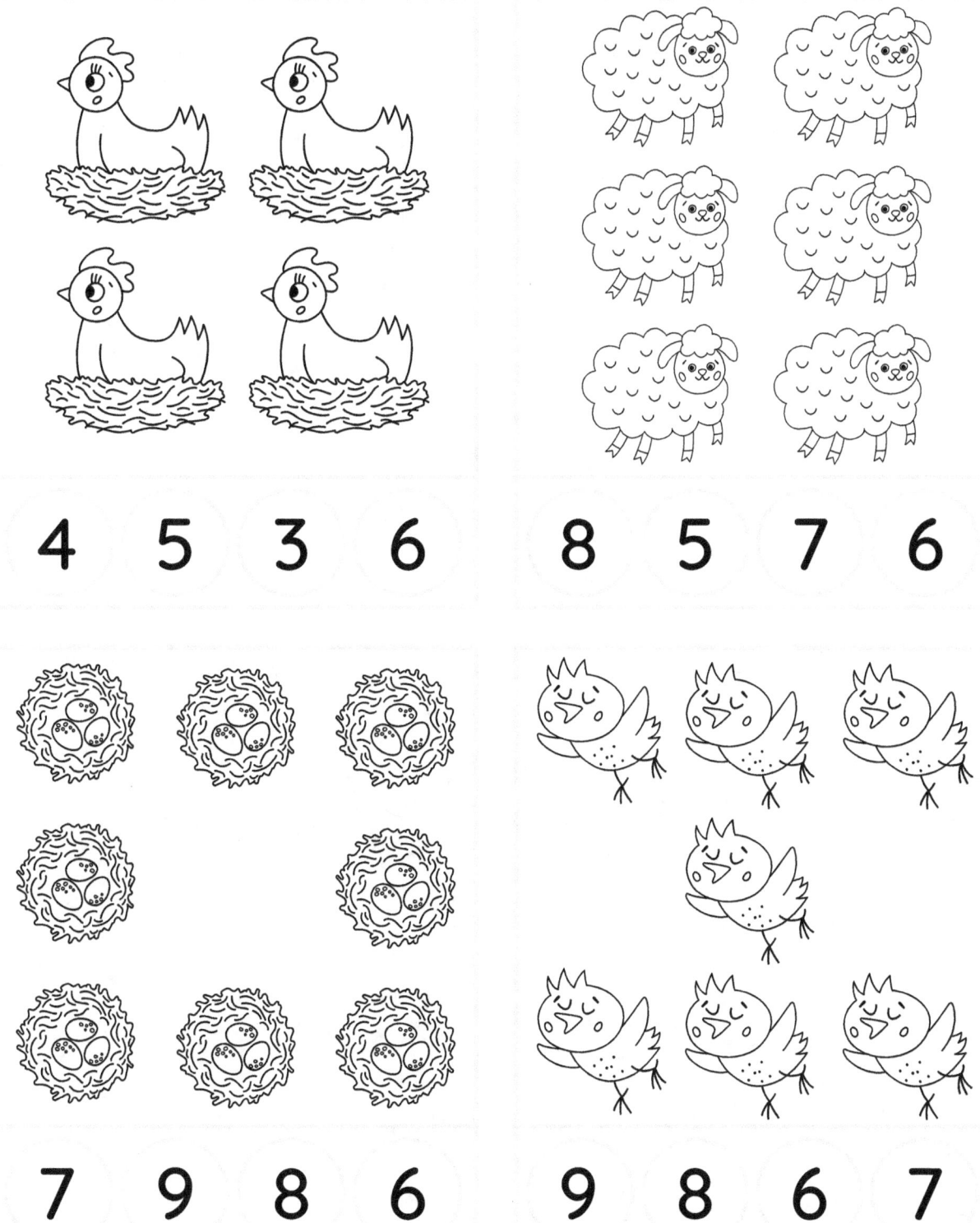

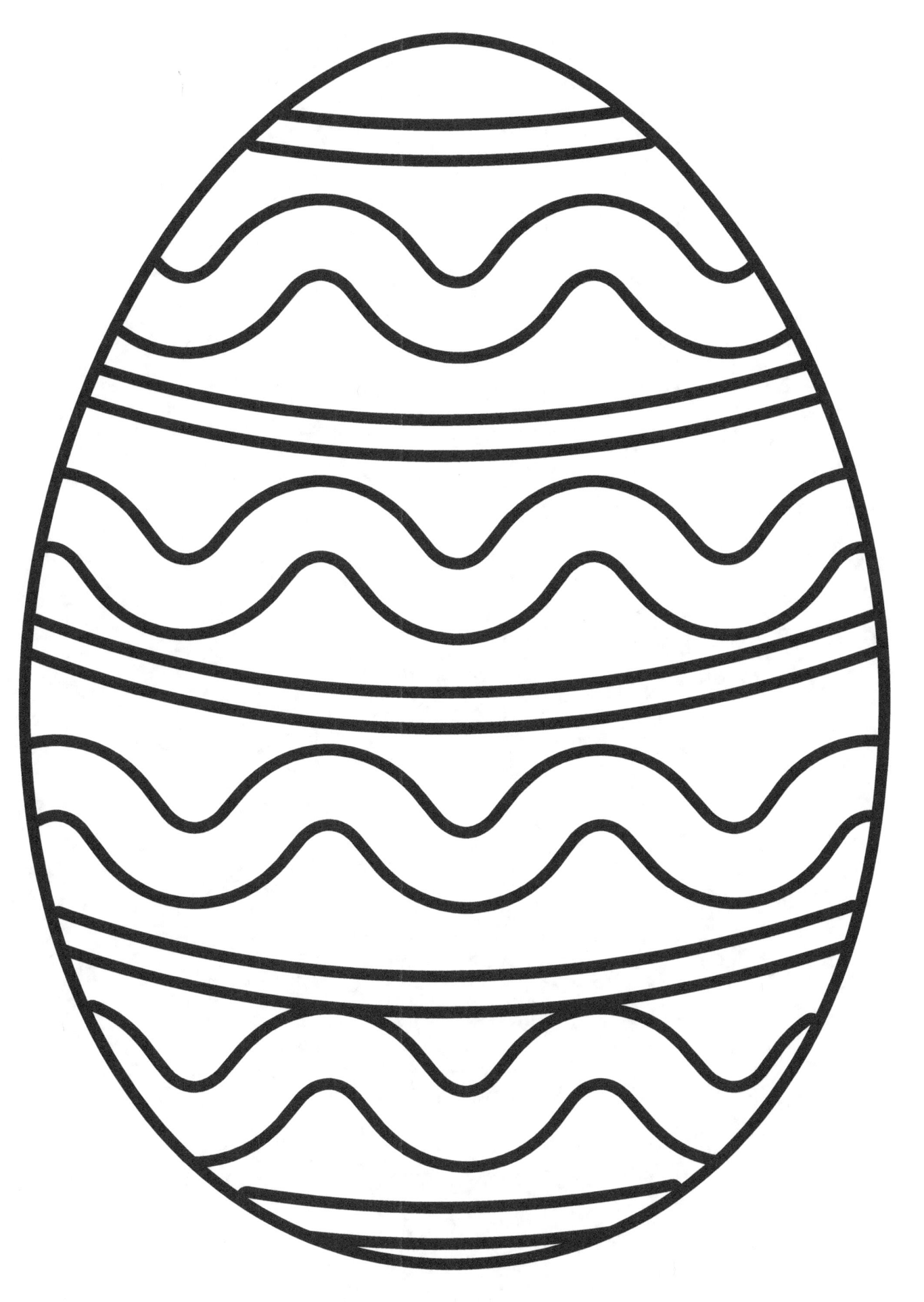

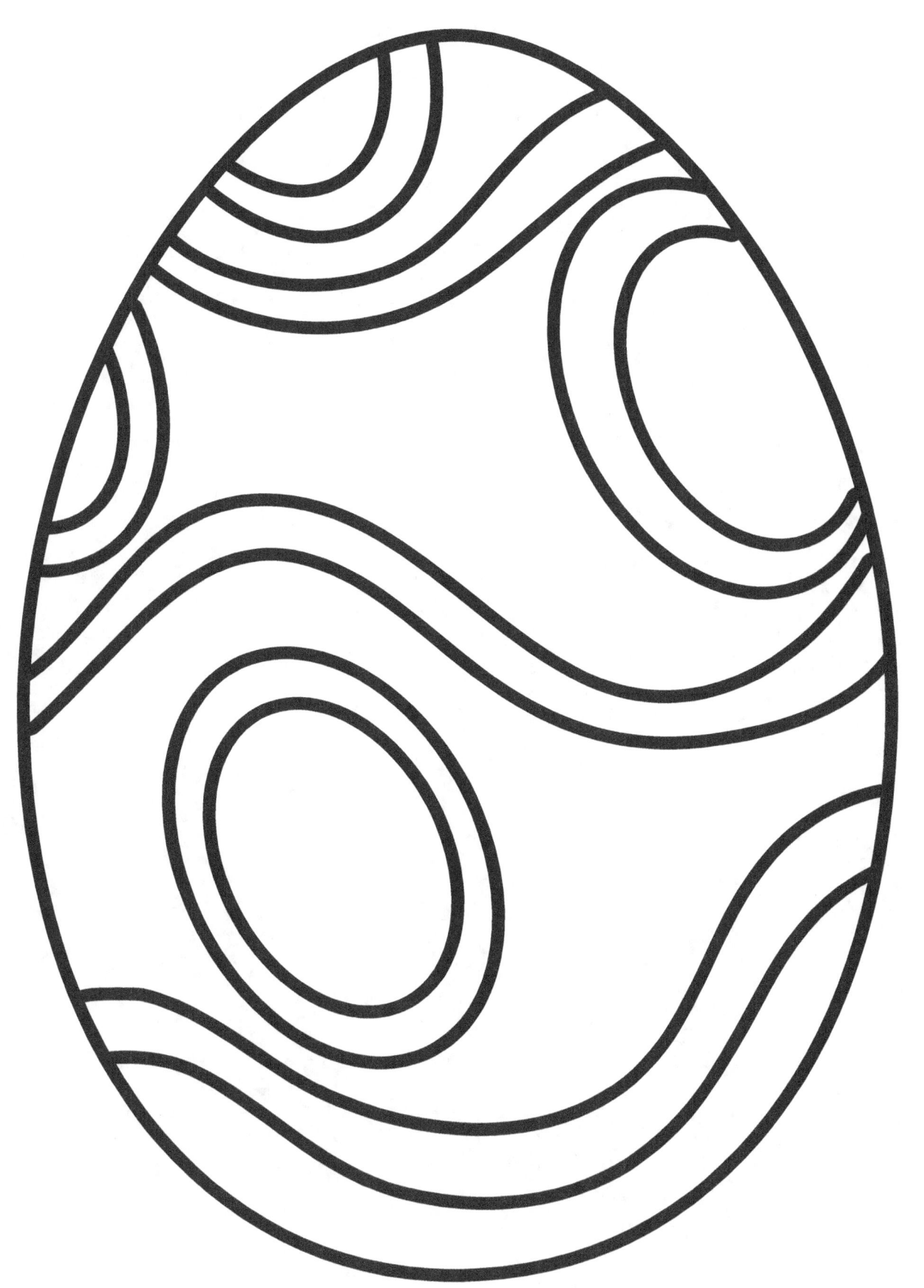

Count & Mark

Count and color the Easter elements in each box,
mark the correct number

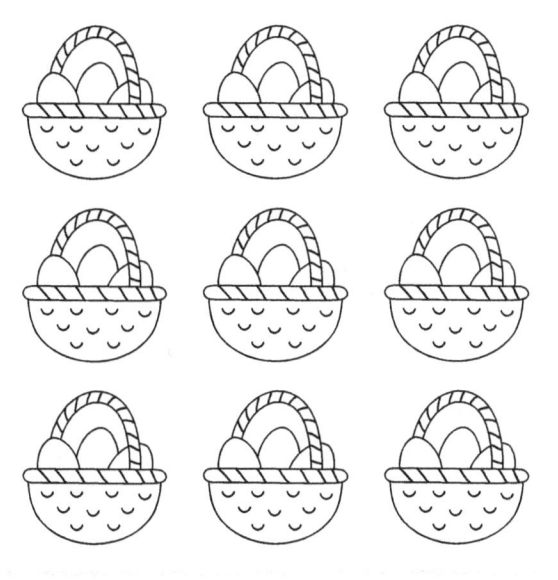

7   9   8   10

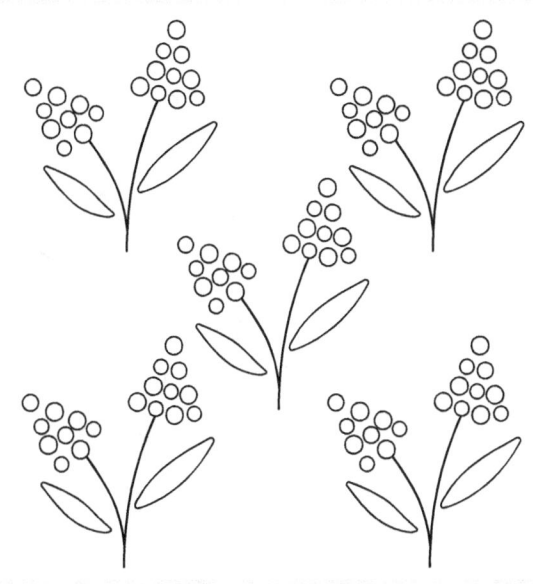

5   6   4   7

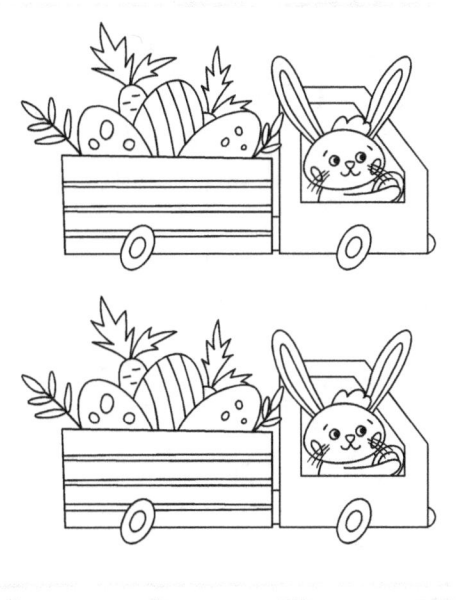

2   4   3   1

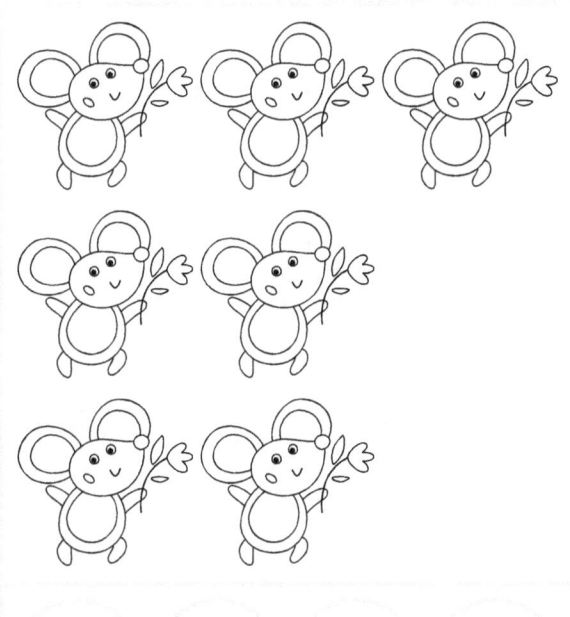

6   4   7   8

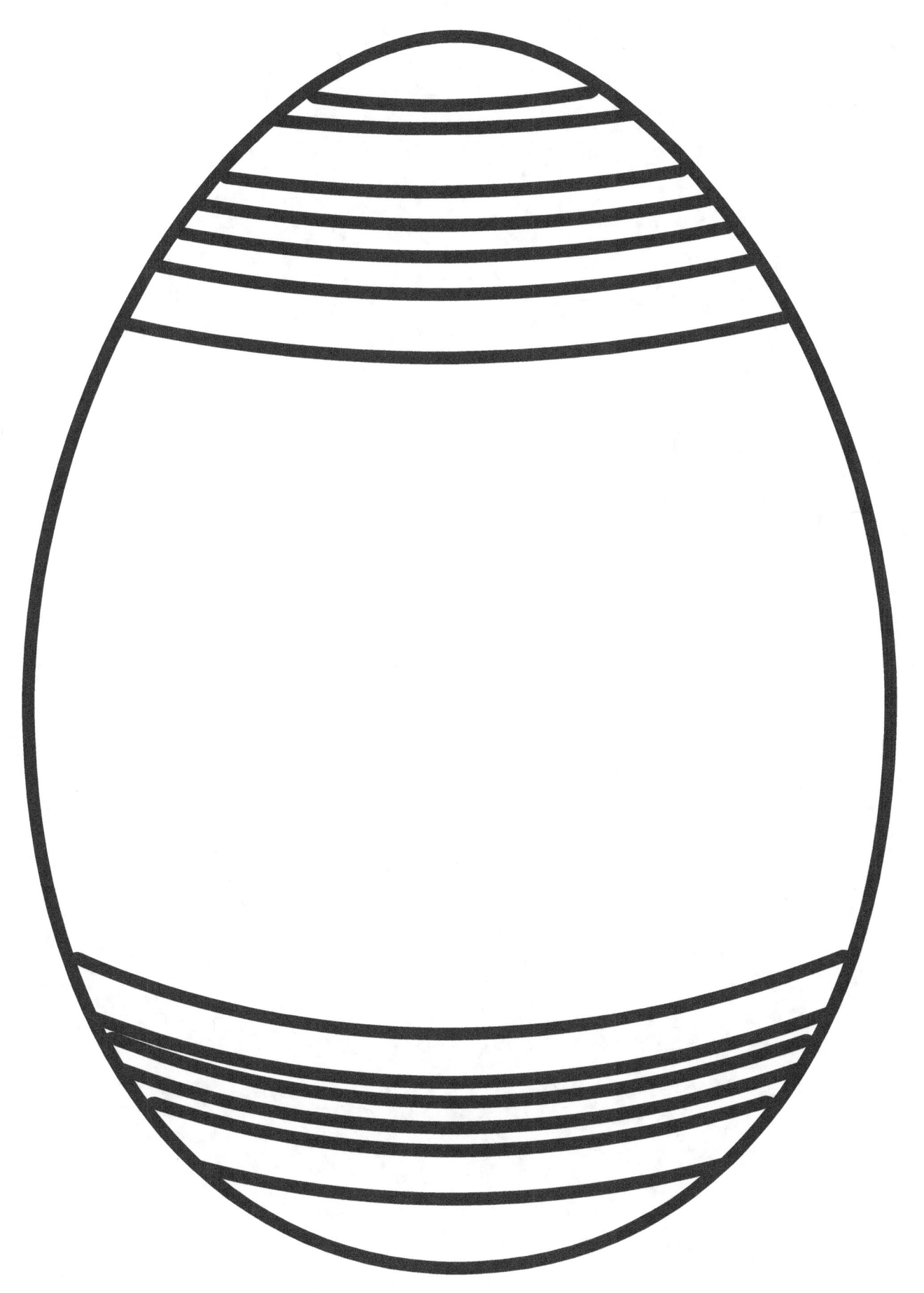

Count & Color

Count and color the exact number of Easter Eggs.

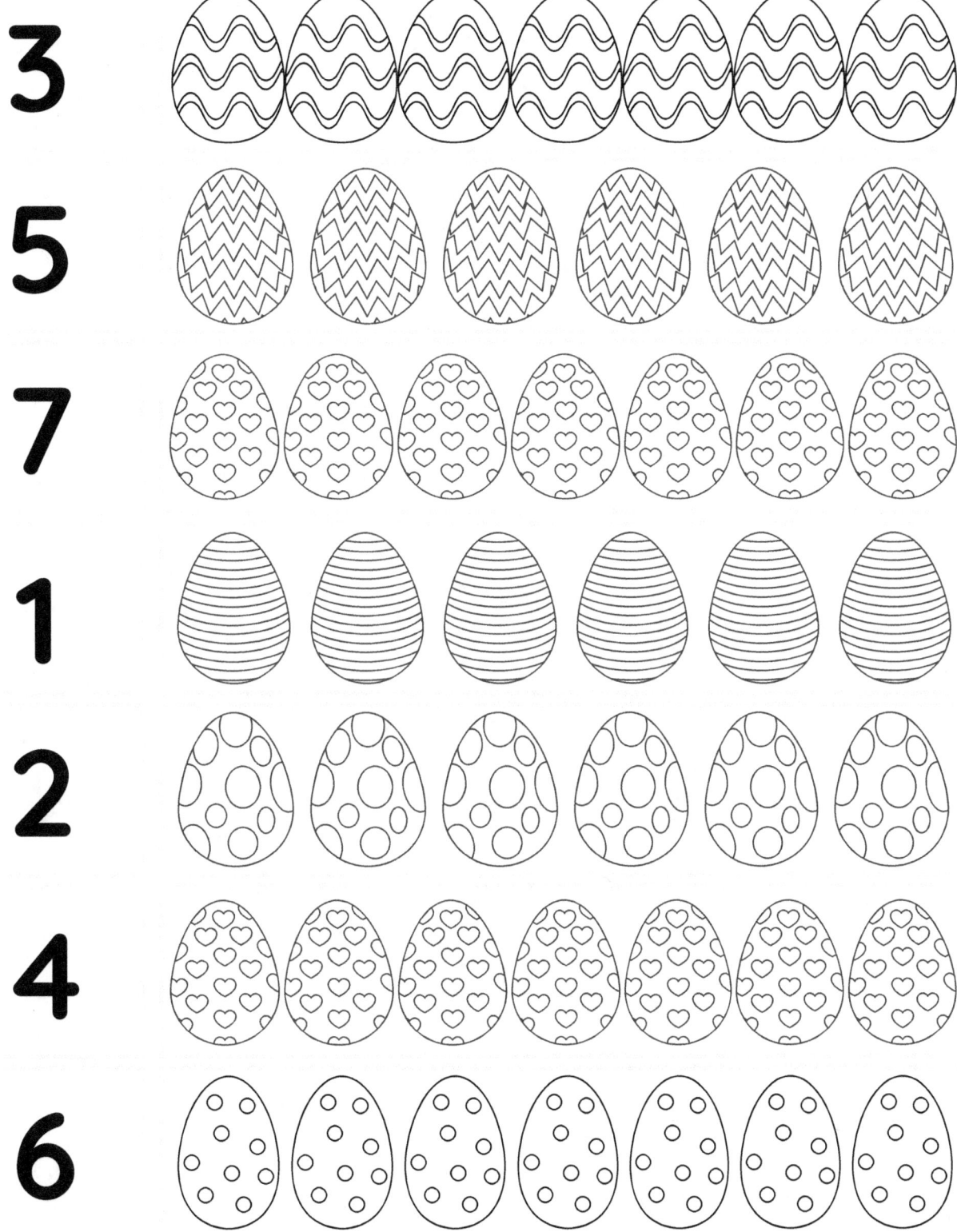

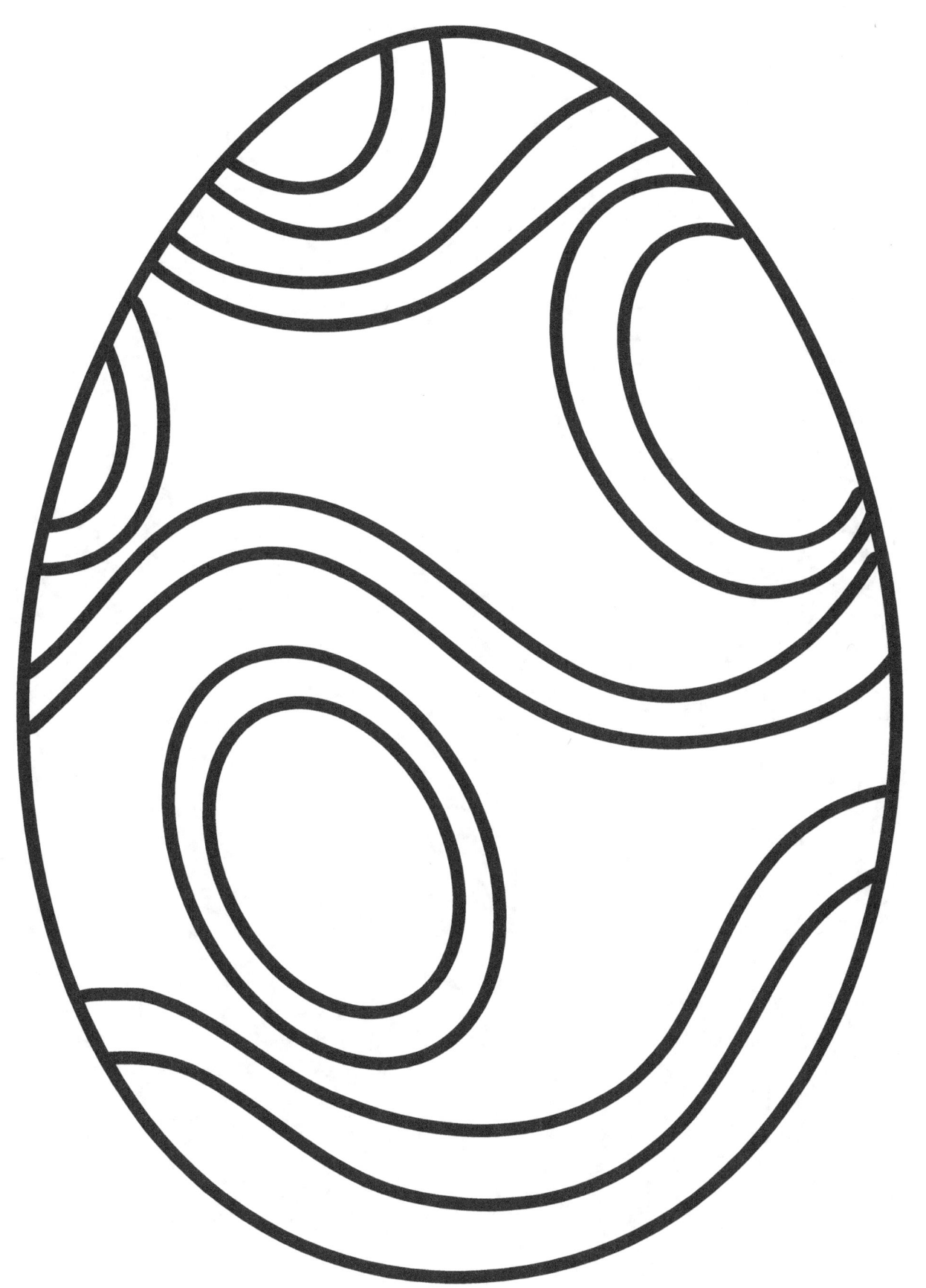

Count & Color

Count and color the exact number of Easter eggs.

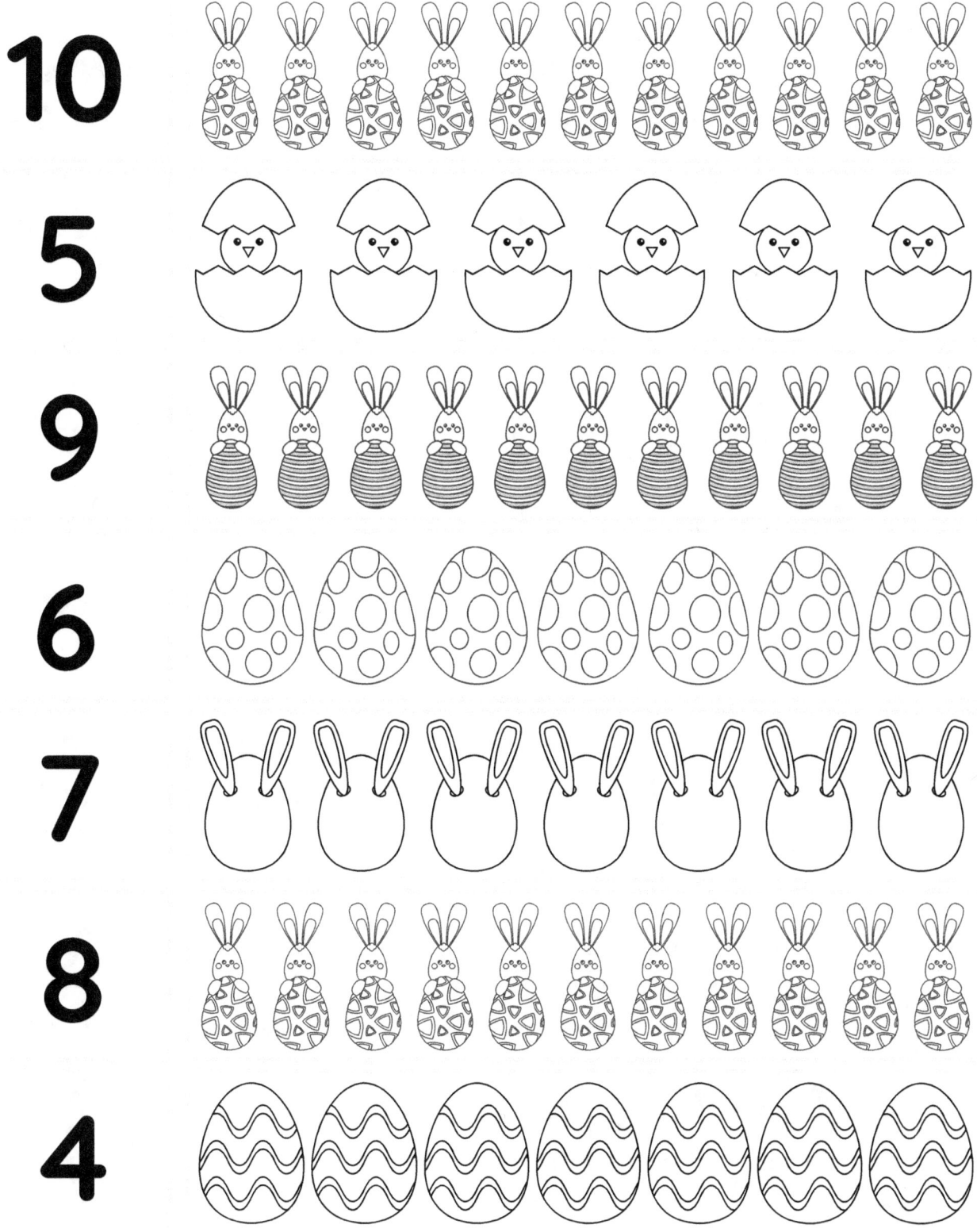

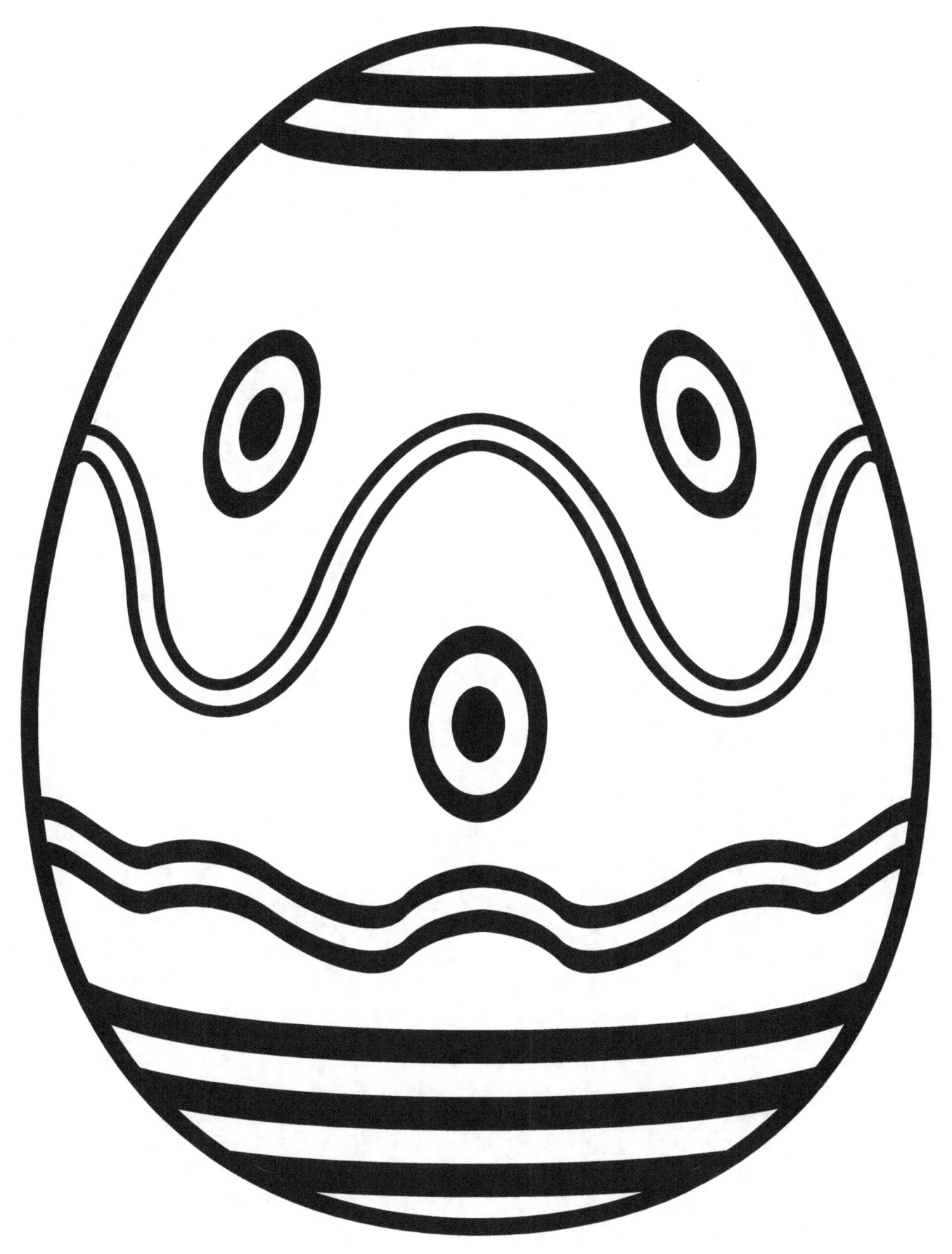

Count & Color

Count and color the exact number of Easter eggs.

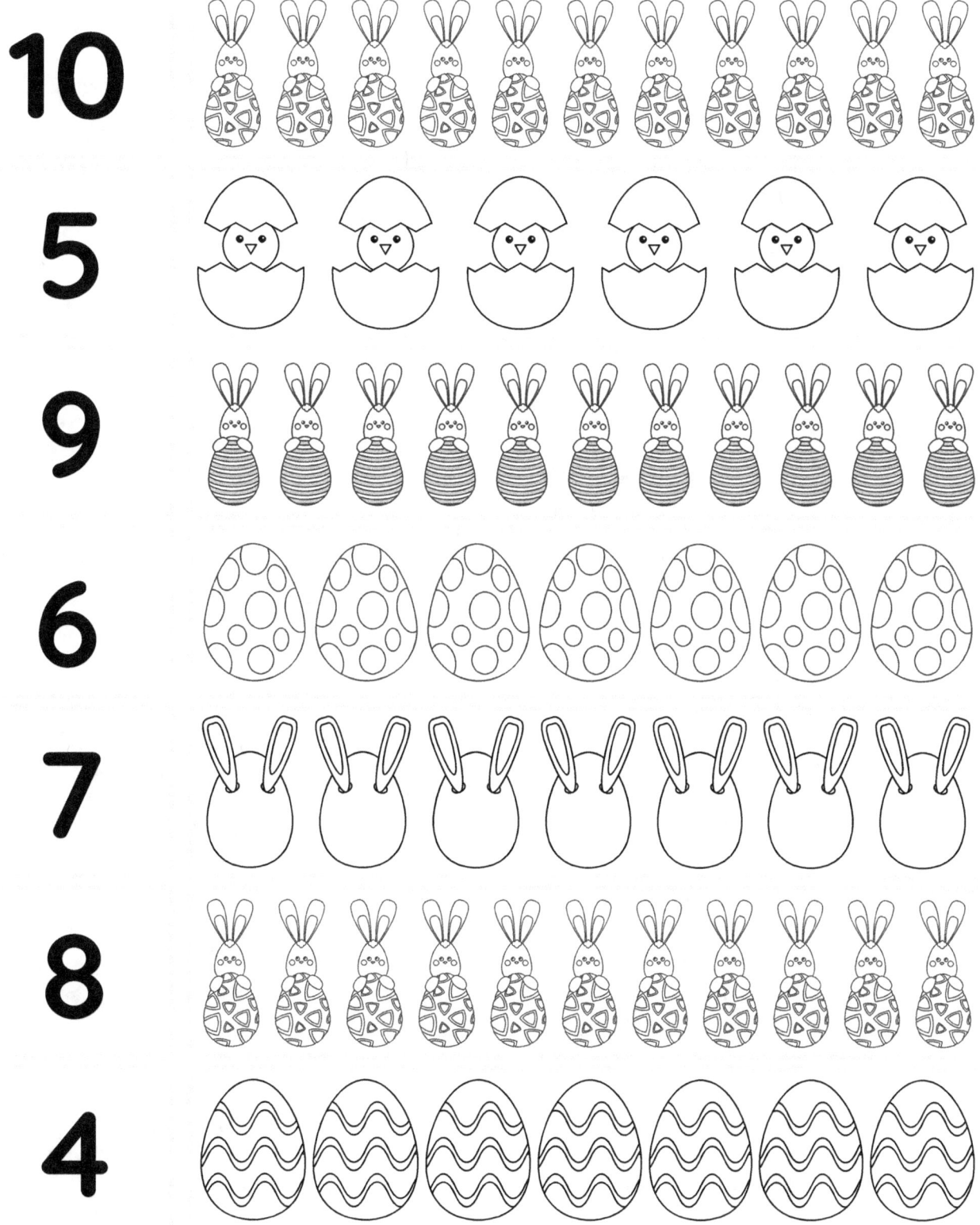

Count & Mark

Count and color the Easter elements in each box,
mark the correct number

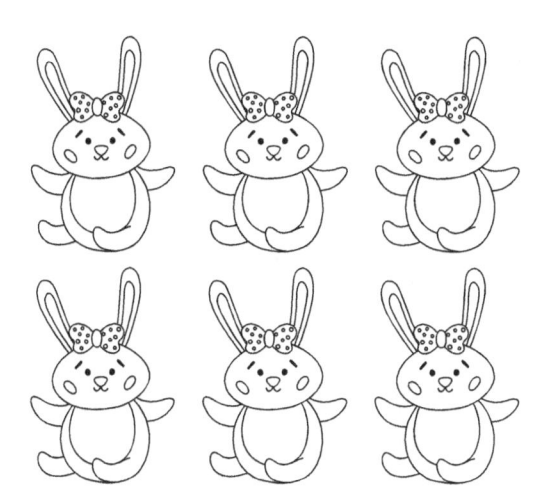
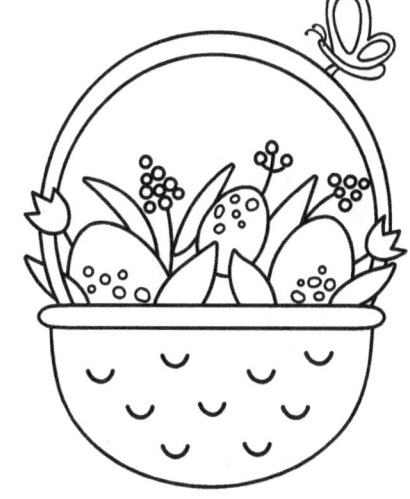

4 7 5 6   1 3 2 5

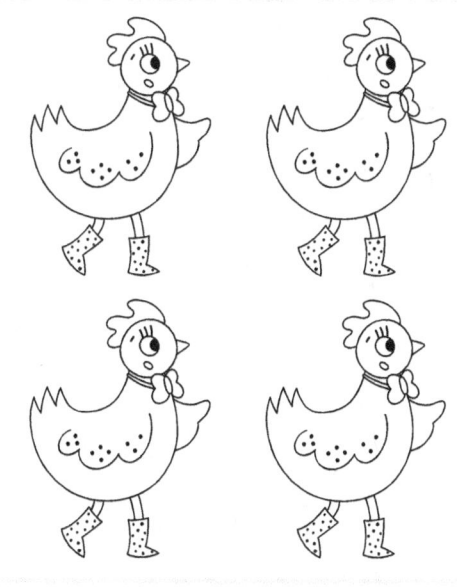
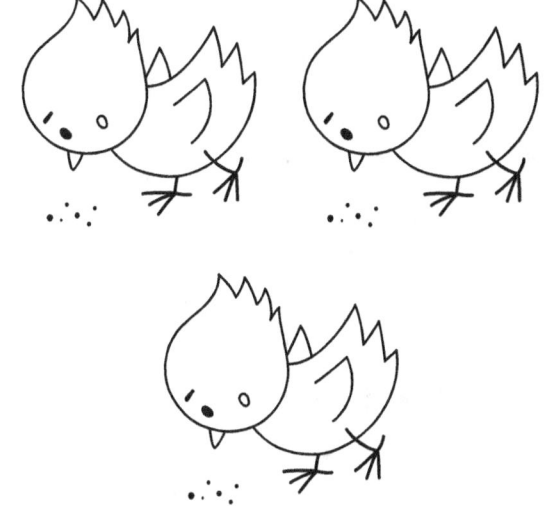

5 4 3 6   2 3 5 1

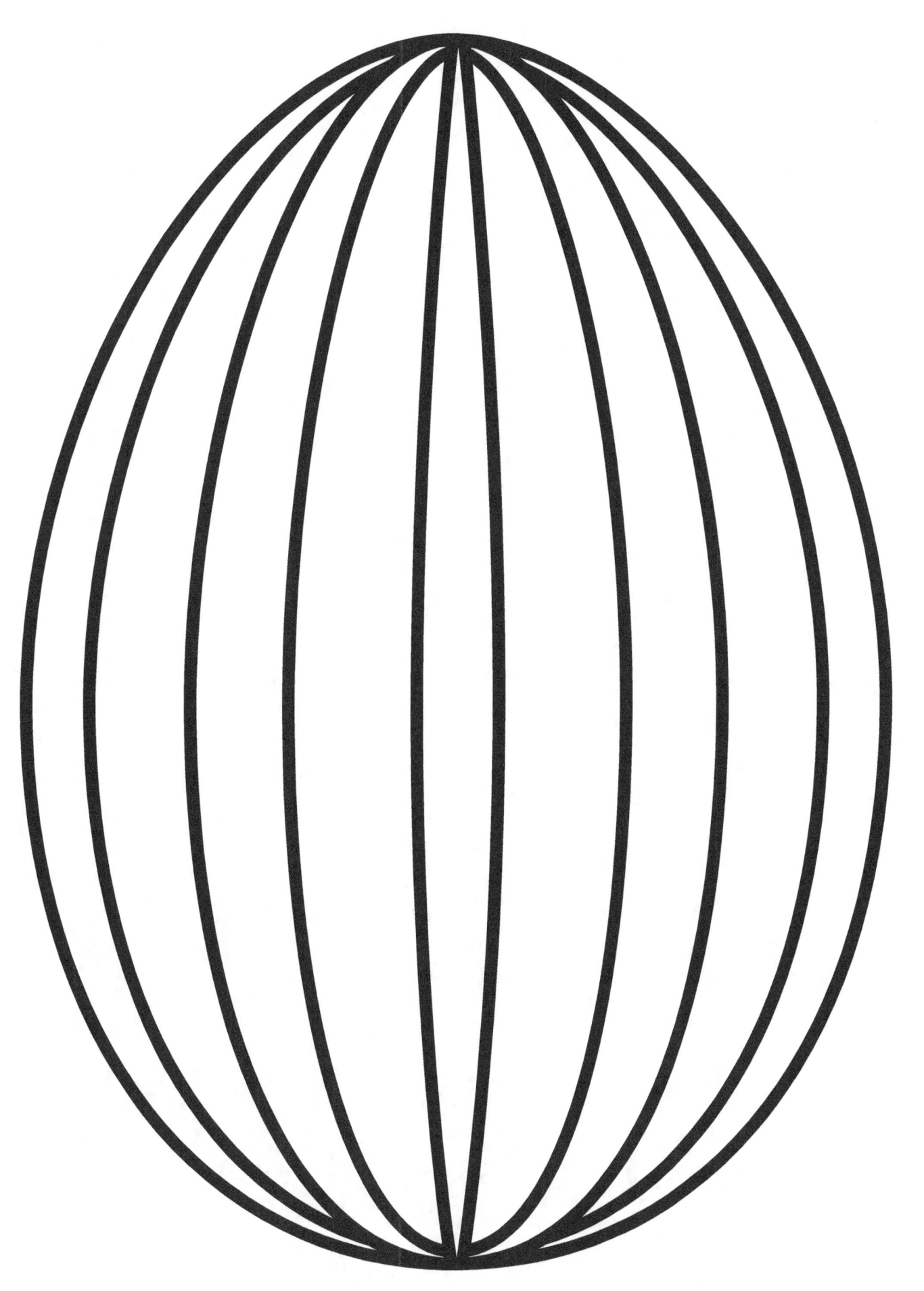

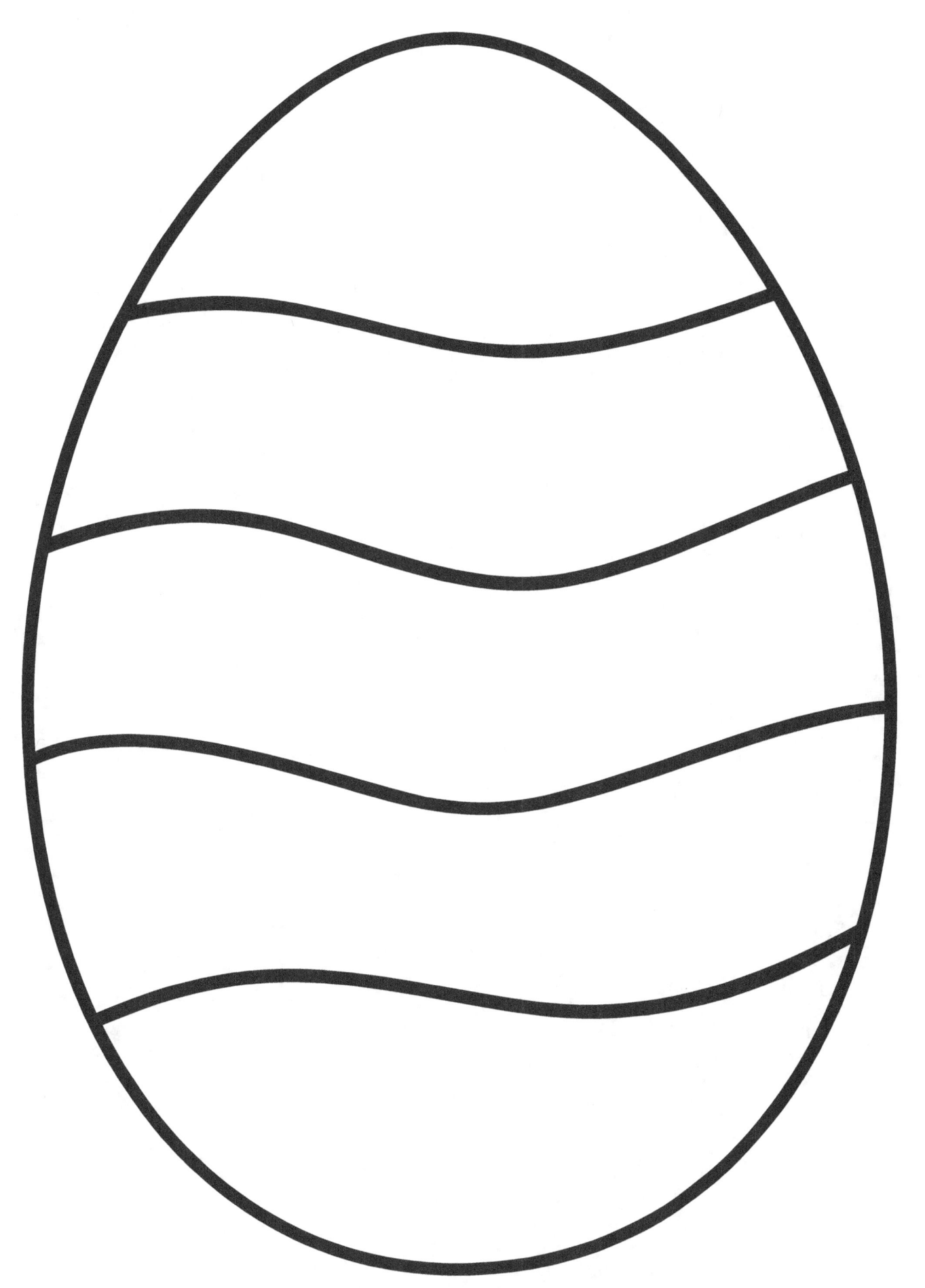

Directions: Color the Easter basket below
Be sure to add some Easter eggs to the basket!

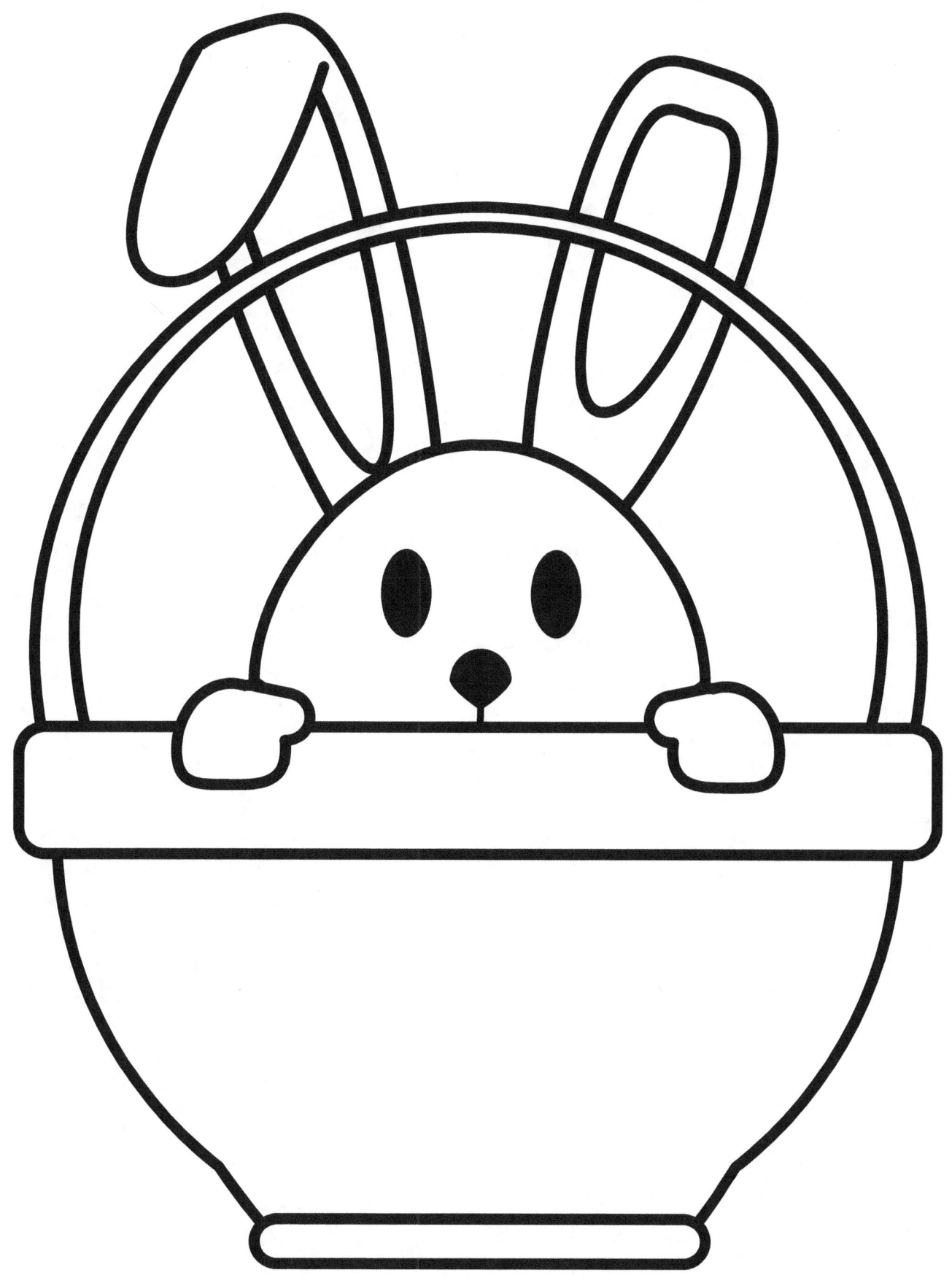

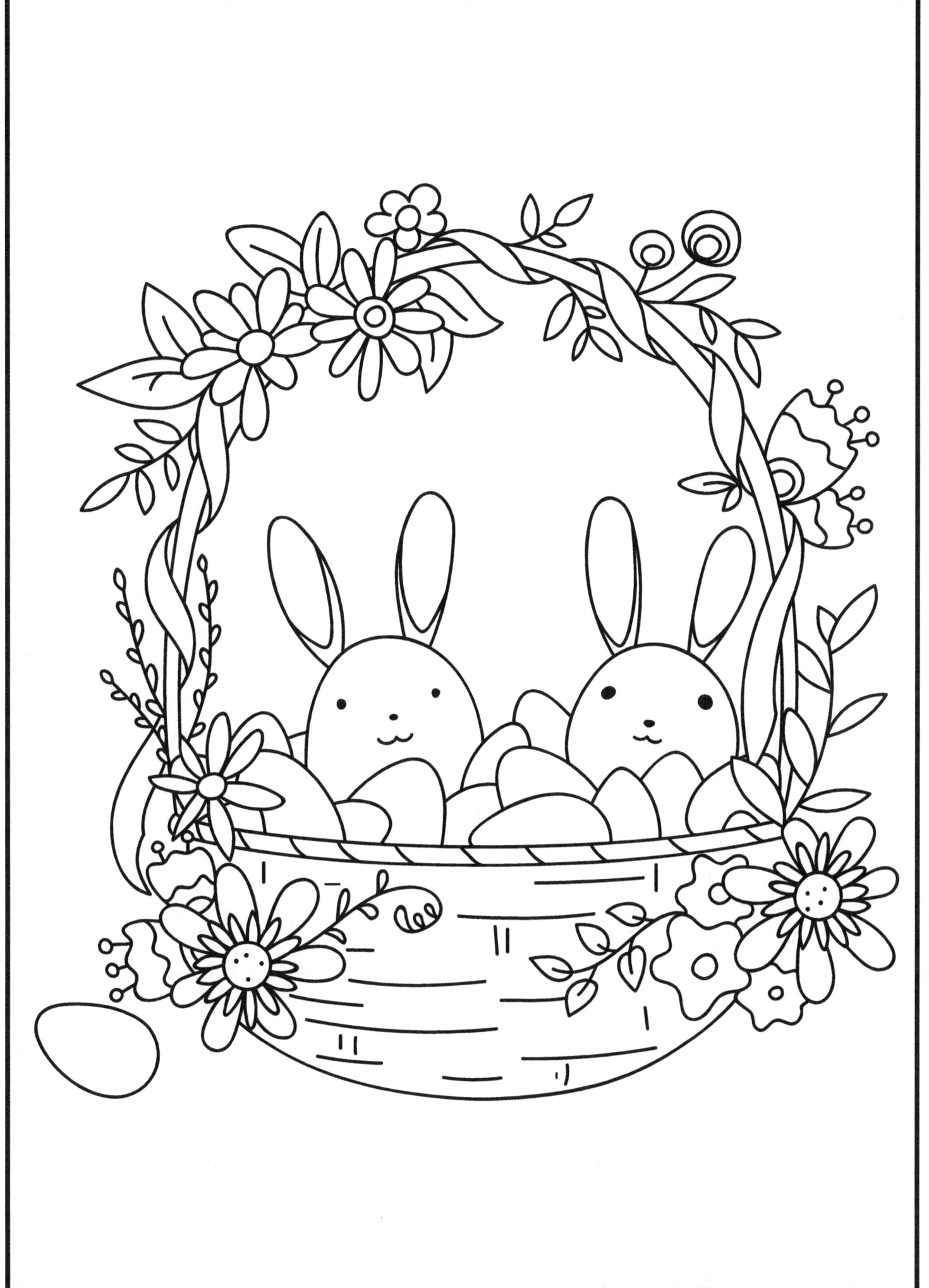

Count & Color

Count and color the exact number of Easter eggs.

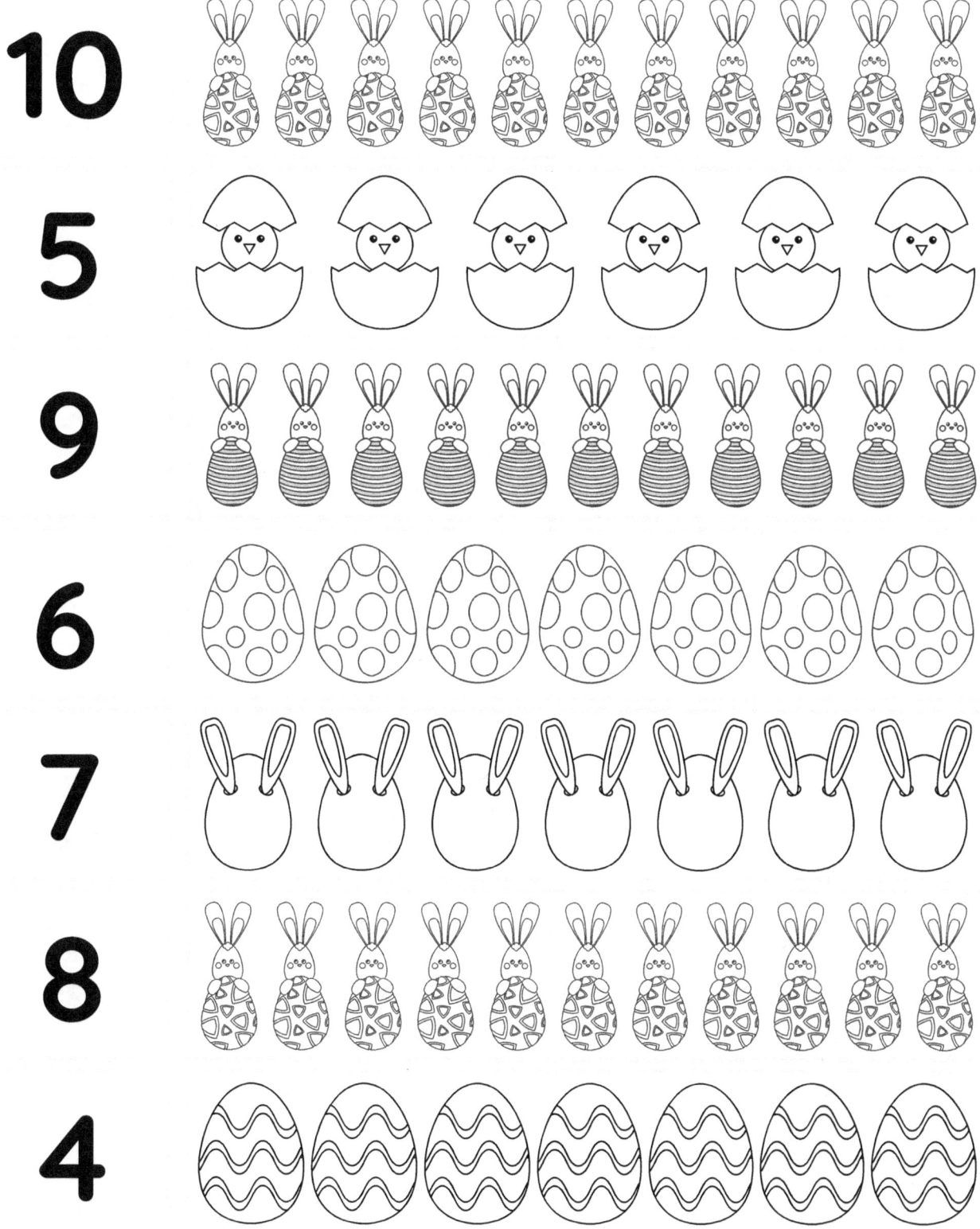

Count & Color

Count and color the exact number of farm animals

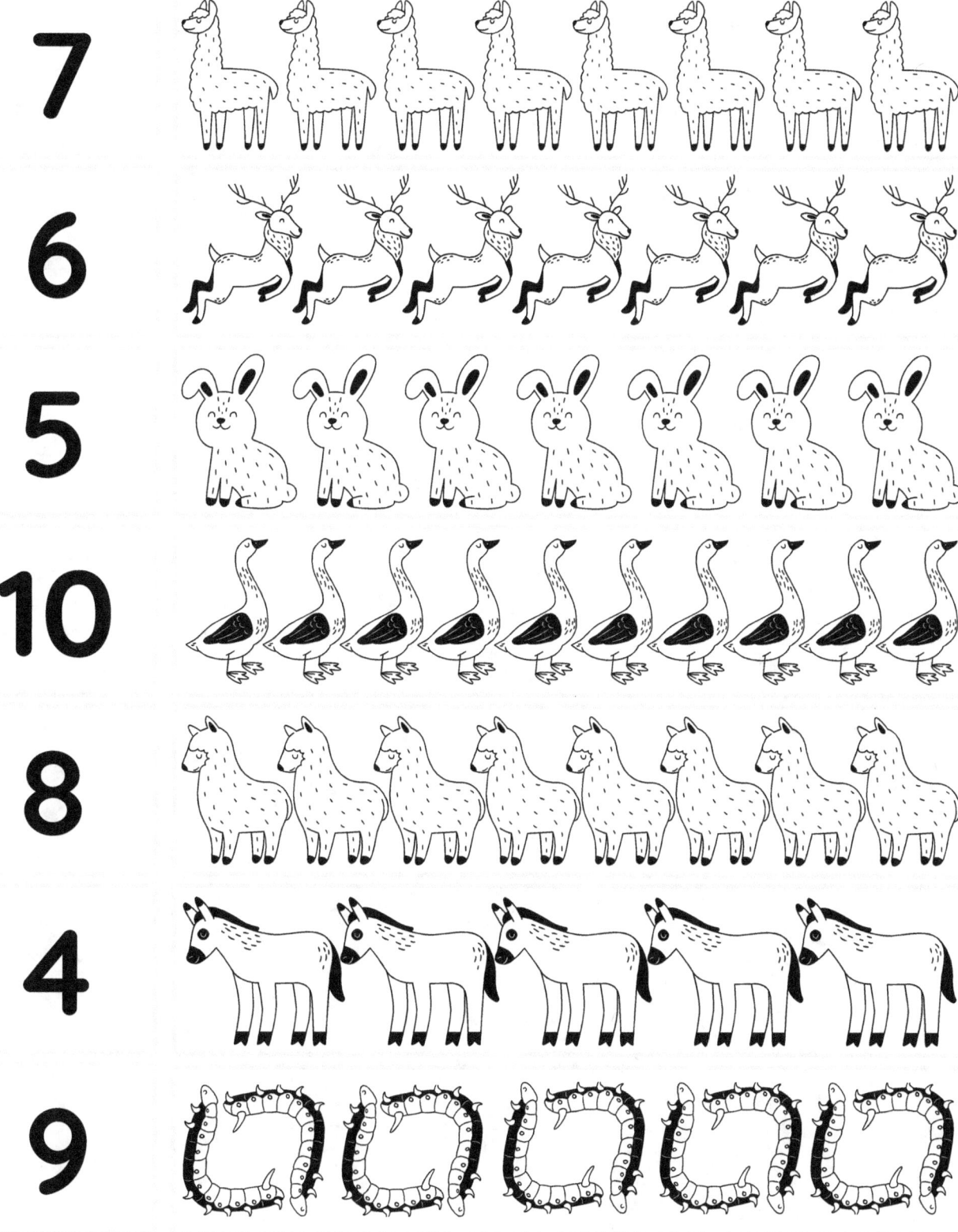

Directions: Color the Easter basket, eggs, and Easter bunny below.

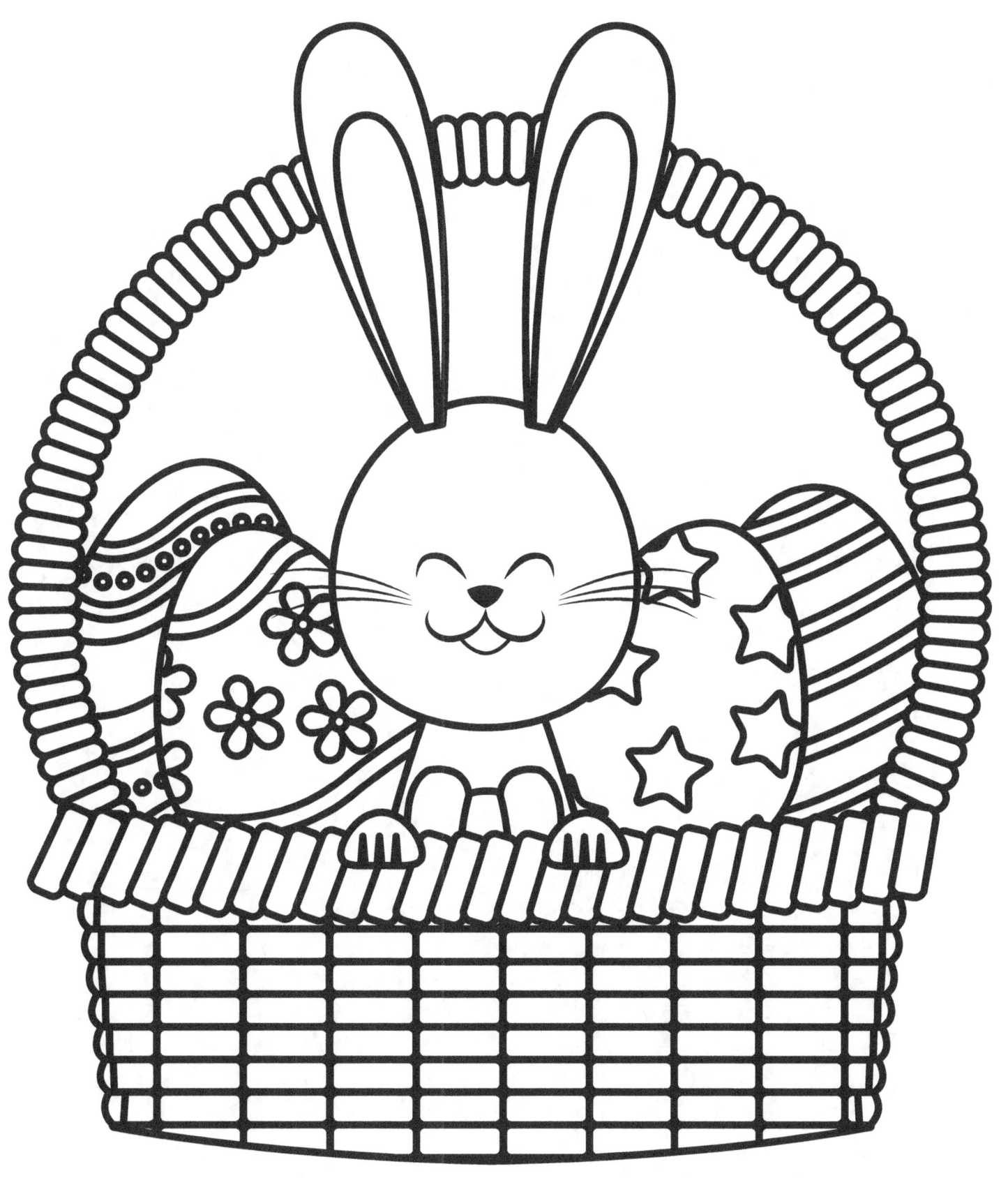

Count & Color

Count and color the exact number of farm animals

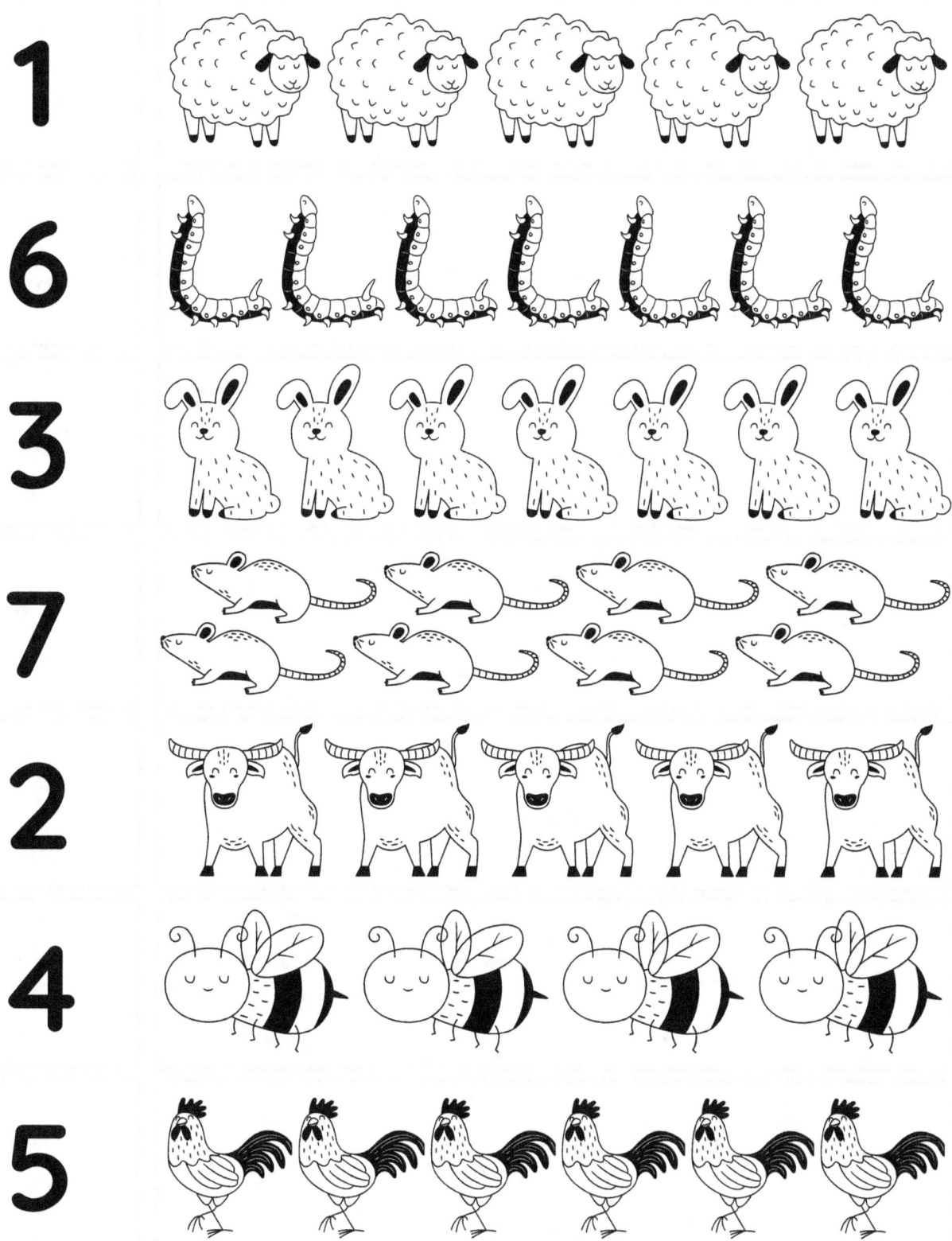

Count & Color

Count and color the exact number of farm animals

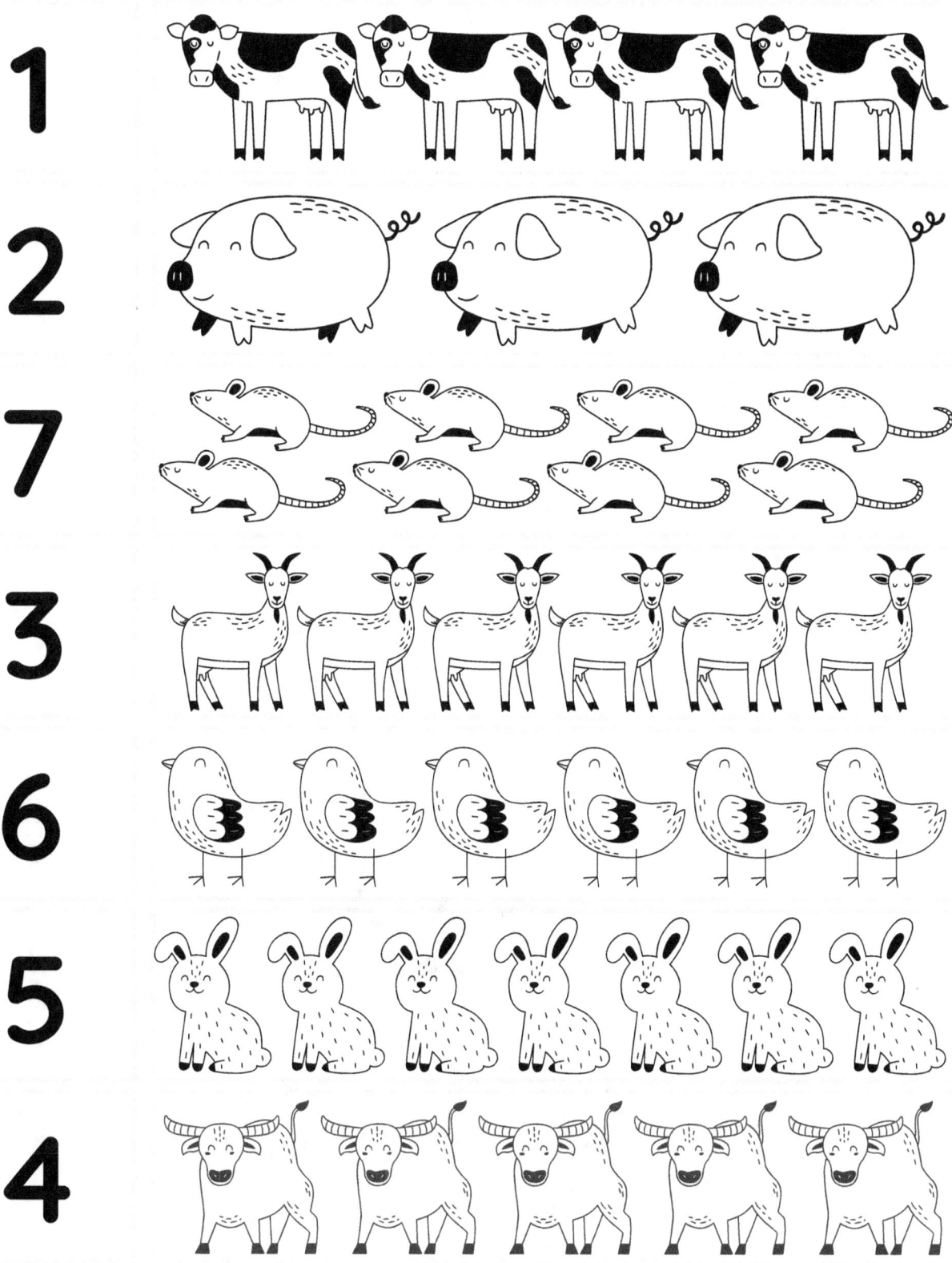

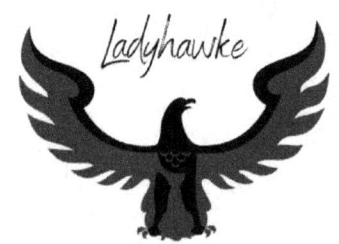

Copyrighted 2022
Ladyhawke Publications
All Rights Reserved

www.ingramcontent.com/pod-product-compliance
Lightning Source LLC
Chambersburg PA
CBHW082116220526
45472CB00009B/2194